Greening Your Family

Lindsey Carmichael

Greening Your Family

A Reference Guide to Safe Food, Personal Care & Cleaning Products

by LINDSEY CARMICHAEL, MPH

PETER E. RANDALL PUBLISHER
Portsmouth, New Hampshire 03802
2009

ISBN: 978-1-931807-92-0

Library of Congress Control Number: 2009931915

Published by:
Peter E. Randall Publisher
Box 4726
Portsmouth, NH 03802

www.perpublisher.com

Book design: Grace Peirce

Cover photography: Jerry Monkman, Grace Peirce

Additional copies available from:
        Lindsey Carmichael
        Box 54, Portsmouth, NH 03802
        www.greeningyourfamily.com

Contents

Tables

Preface

I have written this book for several reasons. Most important, I wanted to create a guide that makes it easy for parents to make informed decisions about the safety of numerous consumable products they bring into their homes. The disturbing truth about many of these products is that they contain chemicals that are potentially harmful to human health, particularly the health of children.

Another motivating factor is to raise awareness about the fact that there are hundreds of toxic chemicals in the products that line the shelves of our supermarkets, big-box stores, and mega-retailers. Most of these chemicals have not been tested for safety, and many ultimately wind up in us and in our children.

Six years ago, when my son was an infant, I was unaware of the extent to which I was exposing him and the rest of my family to products that potentially pose health risks. It was only after an asthma diagnosis for my son, extensive research, and three years of graduate school that I had a handle on the dangers that lurk in many of our household consumable products. I was shocked to learn that in America, more so than in any other industrialized nation, we are often the guinea pigs when it comes to product safety in the cleaning, food, and personal care product arenas.

We do not need to continue to be the guinea pigs. As a society, we can collectively change the status quo. The change can be accomplished in two ways: first by simply purchasing safer brands of products and second by letting those who represent us in Congress know that industry ought to bear the burden of proving product safety. As it stands today, you and I bear the burden of proving the safety or lack thereof of the many products we consume.

The good news is that there are safe options. These options are presented in an easy-to-follow format in the pages that follow. The first section of *Greening Your Family* focuses on food, the second on personal care products, and the third on cleaning products. What you have in your hands is a reliable reference for everything from dishwasher detergent to deodorant.

Refer to the Web site, www.lindseycarmichael. net, for additional information about optimizing the health of your family.

Introduction

My public health ethics class began with the intense, young professor asking a simple question: What do you value the most?

We were given a few moments to reflect, and were then asked to share our answers with the class. Fairly quickly a theme emerged, one centering on relationships with family. For one student, her relationship with God trumped family, and for a few others the idea of freedom was the thing they valued the most, but *people* factored into the majority of responses to the question of what they held most dear.

I think it's safe to assume that for those of us who are parents, our children and their well-being rank at the top of the list of things we value. Collective well-being is what this book is about.

There was a landmark, one-of-a-kind study conducted in 2004 by the people at the Environmental Working Group, a nonprofit environmental research organization based in Washington, D.C. The study was called 10 Americans. Researchers took samples of the umbilical-cord blood of ten babies and tested them for the presence of 413 toxic chemicals.

The results were alarming. More than 285 industrial chemicals were found in the cord blood, with an average of roughly two hundred chemicals per child. The testing revealed the presence of dioxins, volatile organic compounds, Teflon by-products, and pesticides.[1] Exposure to some of these chemicals is associated with a host of serious adverse impacts on human health, including immune and hormone system disruption, attention deficit hyperactivity disorder (ADHD), infertility, birth defects, and cancer.[2] How many of you reading this know a child with ADHD, or have a friend who has had trouble conceiving?

Lobbyists in the industrial chemical industry acknowledge the presence of these chemicals in humans, but they assert that these chemicals exist at extraordinarily low doses, or concentrations, and that therefore any adverse effect on human health is dubious.

Ken Cook, president of the Environmental Working Group, addressed this point in a presentation he gave about the 10 Americans experiment. He talked about the fact that many pharmaceuticals are designed to trigger the desired biological effect at very low doses, and discussed various examples.

The asthma drug Albuterol, he said, is designed to be effective at 2.1 parts per billion. Cialis, the erectile-dysfunction drug, is designed to trigger the desired biological effect at 30 parts per billion. Cook made the point that 97.5 parts per billion of the chemical Badge-40H (found in the liners of tin cans and linked to hormone system disruption) were found in a sample of blood taken from a man living in New York City. The same person registered 45 parts per billion of perfluorocarbons (PFCs), the industrial chemical found in nonstick materials such as Teflon. In studies, PFCs have been linked to both hormone disruption and cancer. Thus, though the concentration of some of these chemicals is minute, their effect is not. The impact of exposure to pharmaceuticals is regulated and well studied; the impact of exposure to industrial chemical cocktails is neither well regulated nor well studied.

The 10 Americans study confirms that babies today are born pre-polluted. We know that the most vulnerable times in human development are in the womb and in infancy. And we know, based on the results of the Environmental Working Group's research, among other sources, that as a society, we are not adequately protecting those who are most vulnerable.

It is time to start. There are numerous steps we can take to reduce exposure to harmful industrial chemicals. To learn how, please read on.

Labeling

Can anyone say what the labels EARTH-FRIENDLY, NONTOXIC, and NATURAL *really* mean? It can be difficult to interpret the meaning behind the wide variety of eco labels appearing on many of the products we buy today. Hundreds of products boast the word *natural* somewhere on their label. However, the word does not necessarily mean that the product is natural. Buyer beware!

Informed decision making is a central theme of this book, and to that end, it's important to be aware of today's labeling landscape in the United States and Canada. To begin with, all products are made from materials derived from the earth, so in a sense, all are natural to varying degrees. Very few chemicals, however, are included in products without some amount of synthetic processing.

Food

Labeling in the food industry is more heavily regulated than is labeling in either the cleaning or the personal care products industry. In the United States, if you see a green-and-white USDA ORGANIC label on a food item, it's an indication that the item is at least 95 percent organic. Not only has the product been grown according to government standards, but the grower has also been inspected by an outside auditor and received a passing grade for compliance with the strict standards detailed by the United States Department of Agriculture (USDA). If an item has a label that reads MADE WITH ORGANIC INGREDIENTS, then consumers should know that at least 74 percent of the ingredients are organic.[1]

It's a different story, though, with the word *natural*. The word *natural* on a food product doesn't hold much weight. It's become a hackneyed descriptor on everything from chips to soft drinks. There is no federal standard for what constitutes *natural*. Consequently, it appears on products that are truly natural as well as products that are not.

If a product is labeled GMO [Genetically Modified Organism] FREE or GE [Genetically Engineered] FREE, then ostensibly the product has not been genetically manipulated. You should know, though, there is no certifying body for this label.

A dairy product with the label HORMONE-FREE indicates that it does not contain synthetic hormones.

The practice of injecting growth hormones into cows (a means of bolstering milk production) has been outlawed in many nations, including Canada, but it remains legal in the United States. One reported consequence of administering growth hormones to dairy cows is an increase in infection of the udder, called mastitis. Often, farmers rely on antibiotics to either treat the infection or keep it at bay. The USDA enforces that dairy products with the USDA ORGANIC seal are free of any synthetic version of recombinant bovine growth hormones.

The label NO ADDED HORMONES, NO HORMONES ADMINIS-TERED, or ANTIBIOTIC FREE on beef indicates that neither synthetic hormones nor subtherapeutic levels of antibiotics have been given to the animals. (Factory farmers will often inject their cattle with growth hormones to make them grow faster.) In the United States, it is not legal to inject poultry or pork with hormones, so any hormone labeling is meaningless on these types of meat. There is conflicting evidence regarding the veracity of the NO ADDED HORMONES and ANTI-BIOTIC FREE labels. Some reports point toward the fact that there is no organization overseeing the claim; therefore, the only avenue to ensure that your meat is free of hormones and antibiotics is to buy meat with the USDA ORGANIC label on it. That label on meat is also an indication that the animals were fed a diet of grass or grain, with no animal by-products in it, and aren't jammed into feedlots.

Labeling guidelines for supplements are not addressed in this book. For more information on supplement labeling, please refer to the Food Labeling section of the USDA Web site.

Personal Care Products

Until recently, the personal care industry lacked any type of regulation with respect to labeling. In May 2008, the Natural Products Association launched a certification program that holds the manufactures sporting its seal to a high standard when labeling their products "Natural." The products must be at least 95 percent natural, contain no ingredients with suspected human health risks, and be minimally processed. As of the writing of this book, the list of companies able to sport the NATURAL seal is short, but growing fast. The seal is round with a green-leaf logo in the center, and reads, NATURAL PRODUCTS ASSOCIATION CERTIFIED. Refer to the Natural Products Association Web site for an up-to-date list of certified products (www. naturalproductsassoc.org).

The natural foods retailer Whole Foods Market launched a personal care products labeling campaign in 2008. In an effort to set a high standard of quality, the people at Whole Foods had spent several years conducting research and reviewing public safety and environmental data prior to introducing their Premium Body Care label. Products bearing this label have been screened to ensure that they work as advertised, the ingredients are minimally processed, the environmental impact over their life cycle is minimal, and the ingredients pose no known risks to human health. This label is round, with two shades of green, and reads WHOLE FOODS MARKET PREMIUM BODY CARE.

More information about the Premium Body Care label can be found on the Whole Foods Market Web site, or pick up a Premium Body Care pamphlet, which is available in its stores. This is a great example of a company working diligently to demystify the process of purchasing safe personal care products.

Cleaning Products

The cleaning products industry is largely unregulated when it comes to labeling. You might see the words *nontoxic*, *natural*, or *environmentally friendly* on a product; however, what's on the label might not match what's inside the bottle. Many manufacturers do not fully disclose all of the ingredients in their products; in these cases a consumer is unable to make an educated decision about the safety of a product. Seventh Generation, Biokleen, and Earth Friendly Products are some better-known brands that do list all product ingredients on their packaging. These brands are a good bet.

If a household cleaning product has a NON-TOXIC, BIODEGRADABLE, or PHOSPHATE-FREE label, perhaps the product won't make you sick and will decompose relatively shortly after it's been used, but know that in the United States, there are no federal standards for these particular terms, nor is there a federal body that oversees the use of them.

If a product is labeled LOW or NO VOCS (volatile organic compounds), it's an indication that it contains VOC concentrations that are below the legal limit set by the Environmental Protection Agency (EPA). The EPA is the federal body that oversees and enforces the use of VOC labeling in the United States.

Design for the Environment (DfE), a partnership program sponsored by the EPA, works with businesses to reduce pollution that may pose risks to people and the environment. If you see a product bearing the Design for the Environment seal, it means the product has been screened for its toxicity, biodegradability, potential for bioaccumulation, and toxic by-products. Cleaning product manufacturers participating in this program do so voluntarily, and it represents a step in the right direction with respect to improving the formulation of cleaning products to protect human health.

For more information, please visit the EPA Web site (www.epa.gov).

Food

We've all heard it before: You are what you eat. It's undeniable that to a degree, the food we consume has an impact on our overall health. According to the World Health Organization, the top causes of death in high-income (which roughly translates to the word *overfed*) countries are heart disease; stroke; cancers of the trachea, bronchus, or lungs; lower respiratory infections; obstructive pulmonary disease; Alzheimer's and other dementias; colon and other rectal cancers; breast cancer; and stomach cancer.[1]

In the United States, four of the top causes of death are closely correlated with diet; these are coronary heart disease, diabetes, stroke, and cancer.[2] This fact is compelling evidence that many of us are making food choices that may have the ultimate impact—premature death.

Michael Pollan wrote an excellent book called *In Defense of Food*. In it he analyzes the forces that have shaped what he refers to as "the Western diet" and provides some sage advice on how to navigate our vast food choices with the best health outcomes.

The Western diet that Pollan describes (the one that kills so many of us prematurely) is characterized by three adjectives: *fast*, *easy*, and *cheap*.[3] Alternatives to the fast, easy, and cheap rut that many of us have fallen into are abundant, but they take planning and effort.

If we want to maximize our health, Pollan's advice is simple: "Eat food. Mostly plants. Not too much."[4] Marion Nestle, renowned nutritionist and the author of *What to Eat,* gives a similar bit of advice when it comes to being healthy: "Eat less, move more, eat lots of fruits and vegetables."[5]

Below are some suggestions for making healthy choices when it comes to choosing food for your family. Later in this section we address individually produce, dairy, fish, meat, and water.

Shorten the Food Chain

Shortening the food chain can be thought of as buying local and growing your own. Often our food travels thousands of miles before it reaches our table. In the case of produce, freshness is diminished and efforts to preserve the shelf life of produce include premature harvesting, chilling, reheating, and treating with gases to facilitate ripening. That's subjecting our food to a lot before it hits the table, not to mention the resources consumed trucking it across the country, for example.

Is there a farmers market in your area? By shopping at one, you will undoubtedly wind up with fresher produce than what is available at the local grocer. Another way to shorten the food chain is to become a member of a local Community Supported Agriculture farm, or CSA. LocalHarvest.org is an excellent Web site to help connect local farmers with local consumers. CSAs are set up such that members pay the farm for a share of the food they produce. The food is either delivered to or picked up by customers on a weekly basis, generally from the spring until late fall. Joining a CSA supports your local economy and helps you to eat well.

Eat Whole Foods

Eating whole foods is a strategy to maximize the nutritional benefits from the food you consume. Whole foods have typically undergone little or no processing or refining, and are more healthful than are their processed counterparts. Numerous studies have confirmed that people who consume diets rich in whole grains have reduced risks of several chronic diseases such as cancer, diabetes, and heart disease.[6]

Buy Organic

What does the word *organic* mean in the context of food? In the United States, if a green-and-white CERTI-FIED ORGANIC seal is on the food, the food was grown in accordance with the standards detailed in the Organic Foods Production Act of 1990. Meats, milk, and produce are 100 percent organic or they are not considered organic. Food items that contain less than 95 percent organic ingredients (breakfast cereals and crackers, for example) cannot sport the USDA Certified Organic seal.[7]

The health benefits of consuming organic food are numerous. Generally speaking, food that is certified organic has been grown in nutrient-rich soils that have been fertilized by manure and compost rather than anything synthetic. Studies have shown that food grown in nutrient-rich soil are indeed more nutritious than is food grown in less nutritious soils.[8] In addition, organic produce is free of synthetic pesticides. There is a laundry list of harmful impacts on human health related to exposure to synthetic pesticides. The endocrine, reproductive, immune, and central nervous systems can be affected; links have been established with lymphoma, leukemia, and breast cancer, as well as other disorders and diseases.

Many farmers today are growing food using methods similar to those spelled out in the Organic Foods Production Act but are not USDA certified.

Certification is expensive and the procedure can be onerous, which may be why some farmers opt not to go through the certification process. This food is often just as healthy as the certified organic food. Farmers who fit this description might be at your local farmers market, or perhaps supply a local produce stand. Don't count these folks out—ask!

CHAPTER I

Produce

Remember Joni Mitchell's "Big Yellow Taxi"? For the younger set, Counting Crows released a popular cover of the song a few years ago. The lyrics make a plea to farmers to stop using the notoriously toxic pesticide DDT:

> *Hey farmer, farmer put away that DDT*
> *now. Give me spots on my apples, but*
> *leave me the birds and the bees. Please![1]*

Upon its introduction, DDT was heralded as a safe way to keep our apples looking pretty. Eventually, DDT was proved to wage war on both human beings and wildlife, and it was banned in the early 1970s. We hope the synthetic pesticides in use today are less toxic than DDT, but there is overwhelming evidence that many of these pesticides are not altogether safe.

The Case for Low- or No-Pesticide Produce

What are pesticides? Pesticides cover a broad range of products designed to repel or kill pests. Some are natural; however, most are altered versions of natural chemicals. In agriculture, farmers use pesticides and herbicides to protect crops from various insects, weeds, and diseases.

Today, many people know about the potential dangers of consuming pesticides, particularly for children. Human exposure to a wide range of pesticides has been demonstrated to have negative effects on the endocrine, nervous, and immune systems. As with exposure to many other synthetic chemicals, children (born and unborn) are particularly susceptible due to their developing systems; their limited ability to detoxify, or excrete the pesticides; and their lower body weight relative to adults. Impacts of exposure may not be immediate. The concentration of a chemical may build up in our bodies over time, and only when the concentration reaches a certain level will the effects manifest themselves. Consequently, it's worth examining your buying habits to minimize the amount of pesticides coming into your home.

There are some excellent resources that are readily available to help us consumers make informed decisions about the food we feed our families. My favorite for produce is the Environmental Working Group Web site (www.foodnews.org). This group of scientists has researched a wide spectrum of environmental issues;

their work on pesticide safety has been compiled into the chart on pages 10–11. Items at the top of the chart have a high pesticide load; items closer to the bottom have a lower pesticide load.

One of the things I particularly like about this list from the Environmental Working Group Web site is that it highlights the fact that pesticide loads vary greatly, and that we don't need to approach produce shopping with an all-organic-or-bust attitude. In fact, I don't buy organic broccoli, onions, avocados, kiwi, or asparagus—I just buy the regular stuff. I don't worry too much because the pesticide load on these particular fruits and vegetables is low. If you are looking for ways to stretch your food dollars while remaining committed to protecting your family's health, this is a strategy to consider.

The FoodNews.org site has a free, downloadable, wallet-size "Pesticides in Produce" guide worth checking out. The same guide is also available as an iPhone app.

Table 1.1 Fruits and Vegetables and Their Pesticide Load

RANK	FRUIT OR VEGETABLE	SCORE
1	Peaches	100 (highest pesticide load)
2	Apples	96
3	Sweet bell peppers	86
4	Celery	85
5	Nectarines	84
6	Strawberries	83
7	Cherries	75
8	Lettuce	69
9	Grapes (imported)	68
10	Pears	65
11	Spinach	60
12	Potatoes (white)	58
13	Carrots	57
14	Green beans	55
15	Hot peppers	53
16	Cucumbers	52
17	Raspberries	47
18	Plums	46
19	Oranges	46
20	Grapes (domestic)	46
21	Cauliflower	39
22	Tangerines	38
23	Mushrooms	37
24	Cantaloupes	34
25	Lemons	31
26	Honeydews	31
27	Grapefruit	31
28	Winter squashes	31
29	Tomatoes	30
30	Sweet potatoes	30
31	Watermelons	25
32	Blueberries	24
33	Papayas	21

RANK	FRUIT OR VEGETABLE	SCORE
34	Eggplants	19
35	Broccoli	18
36	Cabbages	17
37	Bananas	16
38	Kiwi	14
39	Asparagus	11
40	Sweet peas (frozen)	11
41	Mangoes	9
42	Pineapples	7
43	Sweet corn (frozen)	2
44	Avocado	1
45	Onions	1 (lowest pesticide load)

Source: http://www.foodnews.org

CHAPTER 2

Dairy

Conventional dairy products purportedly contain higher levels of antibiotics and hormones than does meat. The short story is that dairy cows produce roughly 20 percent more milk when they are injected twice a month with a synthetic growth hormone. One problem associated with frequent growth hormone injections is infection near the injection site. Another is that the more milk a cow produces, the more udder infections (mastitis) the cow tends to contract: Enter antibiotics used to treat the infections. Cows on organic farms are given neither hormones nor antibiotics.

The Case for Hormone- and Antibiotic-Free Dairy

Debate continues on the health impacts of ingesting diary products that have been treated with growth hormones and antibiotics. There are studies linking the synthetic versions of recombinant bovine growth hormones (rBGH) ingested in milk to increased production of a hormone in humans called insulin growth factor 1 (IF-1). Some researchers have concluded that high levels of IGF-1 can be a catalyst for colon, prostate, and breast cancer cell growth.[1] These types of results indicate that the safest dairy choices, with respect to our health, are organic.

One recent study showed that organic milk contained significantly higher amounts of omega-3 fatty acids than did nonorganic milk. The theory behind increased levels of omega-3 is that organic dairy farms must allow the cows to graze outside, which means the cows are eating significant amounts of fresh grass, which is rich in omega-3. The dietary omega-3 is then passed on through the milk. This is just another reason to opt for organic for your dairy choices.

The table of safe dairy products on page 14 was compiled using data from the Cornucopia Institute's National Survey of dairy products deemed to have best farming practices. For the full scorecard report and to look up regionally distributed brands that received high marks, go to: www.cornucopia.org.

Table 2.1 Nationally Distributed Organic Dairy Products

BRAND	PRODUCTS
Amish Country Farms	Milk products
Ben & Jerry's	Ice cream
Boulder Ice Cream	Ice cream
Cedar Grove Cheese	Cheese
Glanbia Falls	Cheese
Cultural Revolution (Kalona Organics)	Yogurt
Green and Black's Organic—USA	Ice cream
Green Field Farms	Cheese
Heavenly Organics	Condensed milk
Helios	Kefir (fermented cow's milk)
Humboldt Creamery	Ice cream, powder
Julie's (Oregon Ice Cream)	Ice cream
Lifeway	Kefir (fermented cow's milk)
Nancy's (Springfield Creamery)	Yogurt, sour cream, cottage cheese, kefir
Natural Choice	Ice cream
Nature's One	Infant formula
Organic Creamery (DCI Cheese)	Cheese
Organic Valley	Full line of dairy products
Sierra Nevada Cheese Company	Cheese
Similac (Abbott Laboratories)	Infant formula (see report on Cornucopia.org)
Stonyfield (Hood)	Yogurt, milk products
This Land Is Your Land	Milk, goat cheese, yogurt
Thistle Hill Farm	Tarentaise cheese
Wallaby Yogurt	Yogurt, ice cream
Whole Foods Markets	Milk products
Wild Oats	Milk products

CHAPTER 3

Fish

Fish and shellfish provide a number of nutritional benefits. Fish are an excellent source of protein, minerals, vitamins, and unsaturated fat. For all its health benefits, however, fish also has some drawbacks. Pollution from rivers and oceans accumulate in the muscles and fat tissue of fish. Because larger fish feed on smaller ones, the larger fish have higher concentrations of pollution in their tissue. Methylmercury and PCBs (polychlorinated biphenyls) rank at the top of the list of contaminants to be most concerned about in fish.

The Case for Being Selective about Fish

Mercury is a naturally occurring heavy metal that can be poisonous if exposure levels are high. Certain industrial processes release mercury into the air.

When the mercury is deposited into a body of water, it is naturally converted to methylmercury by sediment-dwelling bacteria. Methylmercury is relatively easily absorbed by animals and humans. Studies have shown that there are a host of serious health problems associated with prolonged and repeated exposure to methylmercury.

In humans, mercury attacks the nervous system and the kidneys. Fetuses and young children are at the highest risk for mercury exposure because they are still developing. Among health impacts of high exposure are serious neurological problems, some that share symptoms with cerebral palsy.

PCBs are industrial compounds that were manufactured worldwide until the 1970s, when their production was banned in many countries in response to environmental concerns. PCBs are slow to break down in the environment and tend to accumulate in fatty tissue. Bioaccumulation of PCBs in aquatic organisms manifests in the same way that methylmercury does: The highest concentration of PCBs is found at the top of the food chain. As with methylmercury, fetuses and young children are at the highest risk for PCB exposure. Studies have shown that repeated and prolonged exposure to PCBs causes cancer in animals; consequently, the Environmental Protection Agency classifies PCBs as probable human carcinogens.

Certain fish have been found to have the benefits of being high in omega-3 and having low levels of environmental contaminants (mercury and PCBs). The list below is a general guide from the Environmental Defense Fund Seafood Selector Web page (www.edf. org/page.cfm?tagID=1521). Check with your state or provincial Department of Health for guidance, as there is regional variation in contaminants.

- ✿ Alaskan wild salmon
- ✿ Albacore tuna from the United States and Canada
- ✿ Anchovies
- ✿ Arctic char
- ✿ Atlantic mackerel
- ✿ Farmed oysters
- ✿ Farmed rainbow trout
- ✿ Sablefish
- ✿ Sardines

Below you'll find a list of fish to avoid due to their high contaminant load, particularly for women who are or may become pregnant, nursing mothers, and children. The Natural Resources Defense Council has an excellent downloadable "Mercury in Fish" wallet card. It is both comprehensive and compact; visit: www.nrdc.org/health/effects/mercury/protect.asp to download.

- ✿ King mackerel
- ✿ Marlin
- ✿ Shark
- ✿ Swordfish
- ✿ Tilefish
- ✿ Tuna steak

CHAPTER 4

Meat

The Case for Hormone- and Antibiotic-Free Meat

There is some debate over the impact of meat that has been raised with hormones and antibiotics. Much of the beef consumed in the United States and Canada is given both hormones and antibiotics. The hormones, some of which are naturally occurring, achieve two things: They increase the rate at which the livestock grow and they help animals put on weight more efficiently, which yields leaner beef.

Given the grim conditions under which most livestock is raised on industrial farms, disease is prevalent. Antibiotics are administered as a preventive to disease. Animals are closely confined and often standing in their own excrement. Not only is this a perfect breeding ground for disease, but also the living conditions put stress on an animal's system, which in turn suppresses its immune system, which further increases its requirement for antibiotics. Antibiotics help prevent disease in the crowded and dirty conditions; however, they also fuel the growing problem of antibiotic resistance in humans. Does this sound like a recipe for an appetizing main course?

The synthetic growth hormones given to feedlot cattle are suspected endocrine disruptors. Studies have linked exposure to these synthetic hormones with a variety of adverse health effects, such as damage to the reproductive system, as well as potential increased risk for breast, prostate, and colon cancer.[1] Initially, concerns about hormones in beef centered on the hormones being passed to humans through the meat itself. Now, though, discussions are also focusing on the hormone residue in the animals' excrement. This, of course, leads to environmental concerns and to the hormone residue working its way into water supplies.

As with other areas where public health is concerned, the European Union has enacted a ban on the production and importation of meat derived from animals that were given growth-promoting hormones. The ban was put into place due to concerns over the negative impact on human health that has been observed. The ban went into effect on January 1, 1989. Consider writing to your state and federal representatives to voice your concerns and ask for legislative action.

Recommended meat and poultry products are listed below.

- ✿ Certified Organic
- ✿ Natural, meaning the animals were hormone- and antibiotic-free and fed no animal by-products

CHAPTER 5

Water

Clean drinking water is a key component to good health. There are ongoing debates about the quantity of water we should drink and the types of water we should drink. Choices abound: filtered water, bottled water, fizzy water, water from continents far away, and plain old tap water.

With the health of the public in mind, Marion Nestle, author of *What to Eat*, believes the jury is still out with respect to which is better for you: tap water or bottled. Neither is pure. Most municipal water supplies keep microbial contamination below thresholds considered harmful. In most developed nations, chlorine is used to keep the microbial contamination to a minimum. This helps kill off the bugs, such as *Giardia*, that can make us sick.

The Case for Filtering Water

According to scientists who study tap water disinfection, when chlorine reacts with other chemicals present in tap water, it creates by-products that have a negative impact on human health. Two of these by-products are total trihalomethanes (TTHM) and haloacetic acids (HAA), which are created when chlorine and naturally occurring organic compounds mix. Examples of the potential negative impacts on human health are reproductive problems and cancer of the bladder as well as of other organs.

Unfortunately, chemical contamination of tap water doesn't begin and end with chlorine. Hormones, plasticizers, antibiotics, fire retardants, and pesticides have also been found in water supplies.

In our house, for a number of years we bought case after case of bottled water. We were slow to recognize that this practice was a senseless waste of a lot of things, beginning with cold hard cash and ending with the resources required to make the plastic bottles and transport them from the factory to the door. Eventually, we had a good water-filtration system installed under the sink. Four Sigg bottles later, most of us in the house were weaned off bottled water.

Installing a water-filtration system is potentially a great thing to do for your family's health. These systems are available for a few hundred dollars. First, it makes sense to look into the quality of the water flowing from your tap. Depending on the source of that water, you may want to either review your current water-quality report if your water source is public or purchase a water test kit if your water source is private. The results of the water test will reveal whether your water contains contaminants—typically heavy metals and chlorine—that are easily removed using a filter.

CHAPTER 6

Genetically Modified Organisms

Genetically modified organisms (GMOs) are the product of the genes from one species being forced into the genes of another species.[1] An example is taking the genes from an arctic flounder and splicing them into a tomato, the result of which is a frost-resistant tomato.

The Case for GMO-Free Food

The concept is interesting, but the long-term effect of human consumption of GMO food is not yet fully understood. This type of genetic engineering is complex because genes do not work in isolation and the impact of this manipulation is unpredictable. In fact, GMOs have been "linked to thousands of toxic or allergic type reactions, thousands of sick, sterile, and dead livestock and damage to virtually every organ and system studied in lab animals,"[2] according to the GMO expert and author Jeffrey Smith.

The USDA has chosen not to regulate the use of GMOs in our food supply. Consequently, we are the subjects of the uncontrolled GMO food experiment. In many cases, most of us are not even aware that we are participants! The regulatory landscape in this arena is much the same for Canadians. Food manufacturers in the European Union and Japan have committed to avoiding the use of GMOs in their products, and the natural foods industry in the United States is working to remove all genetically modified ingredients from its products.

Products that have been verified to contain no known genetically modified ingredients will sport a GMO-FREE label. Worth mentioning, however, is that GMO crops can contaminate nearby crops that are GMO-free. This happens when pollen from the GMO crop is carried by the wind to the GMO-free field, resulting in cross-pollination.

Here are some guidelines for avoiding genetically engineered foods:

- ☼ Buy certified organic produce.
- ☼ Buy certified organic dairy.
- ☼ Avoid conventional soy, corn, canola, and cottonseed oil.
- ☼ Avoid products containing NutraSweet or aspartame.
- ☼ Buy meat, poultry, and eggs that have been fed organically grown feed.
- ☼ Limit processed foods.
- ☼ Don't buy unless the item has the GMO-FREE label.

Personal Care Products

If ever there was a glaring hole in legislation on the books in the United States, it is in the area of regulation for personal care products. In the United States, personal care products fall under the broad umbrella of the Food and Drug Administration (FDA). The industry, however, is largely unregulated. As things stand today, the FDA has no authority to require personal care product safety testing.

Because of the lack of government oversight, many personal care products contain ingredients known to pose risks to human health. Examples of harmful ingredients that are ubiquitous in personal care products are parabens and phthalates

(pronounced THAY-lates). These two groups of synthetic chemicals have been linked to a long list of
health issues ranging from reproductive toxicity to
cancer.[1]

One of the reasons we should be particularly concerned about ingredients like parabens and phthalates
in personal care products is that most of them are
applied to our skin. Although the skin may look like
a barrier, it does not behave like one. Skin absorbs as
much as 60 percent of what is applied to it.[2] There
are a slew of pharmaceuticals designed to be applied
directly to the skin, such as medicated creams and the
nicotine patch. The ingredients in many personal care
products are absorbed into the bloodstream in the
same way that nicotine is absorbed from the patch.

Unfortunately, the story doesn't end here. A por-
tion of these products is introduced into the environment, through either excretion, bathing, or product
disposal, where they create a secondary set of problems. We have started to see some of these ingredients showing up in our water supplies. These findings
reinforce the fact that we live in an increasingly inter-
connected world. We think we can flush away or
throw away these products, but we can't. As Donella
Meadows wrote in her book *Global Citizen*, "There's
no 'away' to throw things to."[3]

The primary source of information in the personal care section of this book comes from the
work conducted and published by the Environmental
Working Group (EWG). Its Skin Deep Cosmetics Safety

database (www.cosmeticsdatabase.com) is an excellent resource for determining the safety of thousands of personal care products.

The database represents the efforts of the team in analyzing more than 40,000 personal care products. Each product in the database is assigned a Hazard rating between 0 (Low Concern) and 10 (High Concern). The Cosmetics Database Web site includes a detailed explanation of its ranking system. (There are some cases in which a product is assigned a high hazard ranking despite being void of ingredients that could pose a risk to human health, so it also makes sense to hone your label-reading skills.) The Cosmetics Database Web site itself is a unique and extraordinarily valuable tool. It's also very easy to use. I strongly recommend bookmarking the site and telling your friends about it!

There are a few other resources worth referring to that have excellent information about personal care products. One is the Beauty with a Conscious Awards list, compiled by *Natural Solutions* magazine in 2008. Editors worked with the grocery retailer Whole Foods Market to identify companies making shampoos, makeup, lotions, and so on, that contain the healthiest ingredients possible. The list contains more than one hundred companies and is available from the Natural Solutions Web site (www.naturalsolutionsmag.com).

A table of the top fifteen products to steer clear of in your personal care products appear on pages 30–31. *Natural Solutions* magazine and Whole Foods

Market worked together to develop this list. It can be downloaded in .pdf form at this Web address: http://www.care2.com/greenliving/top-15-dangerous-ingredients-in-skin-care.html. An expanded version can be found in the "Quality Standards" section of the Whole Foods Market Web site.

Top 15 Ingredients to Avoid

INGREDIENT(S)	NOTES
Synthetic fragrances	Generally contain phthalates, appear as the word *fragrance* on labels
Parabens	Hormone disruptors
Ureas	Might appear as diazolidinyl urea, DMDM hydantoin, or imidazolidinyl urea, and sodium hydroxymethyl-glycinate
1,4 dioxane	Might appear as ceteareth, laureth, myreth, oleth, oxynol, PEG, polyethylene, polyethylene glycol, or polyoxyethylene
Petrochemicals	Nonrenewable resources that can clog pores
MEA/DEA/TEA	Ammonia compounds; can form carcinogenic secondary compounds when mixed with air and other ingredients in a product
Sulfates	Harsh eye and skin irritants
Chemical sunscreens	Oxybenzone and octyl methoxycinnamate, linked with endocrine system disruption
Quats	Quaternary ammonium compounds; evidence points to their causing skin and respiratory irritation
Antibacterial compounds	Contribute to bacterial resistance and are harsh on the environment

INGREDIENT(S)	NOTES
Synthetic polymers	Manufacturing creates toxic by-products (examples are carbomer and sodium polyacrylate)
Synthetic colors	Labeled FC&C or D&C; suspected carcinogens
Chelators	Slow to biodegrade
Nanos	Questions about the safety of cosmetics that use nanotechnology
Animal testing	Results in millions of animals being blinded, poisoned, and killed every year

Source: http://www.care2.com/greenliving/top-15-dangerous-ingredients-in-skin-care.html

CHAPTER 7

Children's Personal Care Products

Children are uniquely vulnerable to many of the synthetic ingredients in personal care products. The reasons for this are numerous.

To begin with, their skin is thinner and more absorbent than is adult skin, which means that soap, lotion, and shampoo products applied to their skin are more readily absorbed into their bodies. Children's biological systems, such as their endocrine, reproductive, and immune systems, are in a delicate developmental period. Exposure to certain chemicals can interfere with the healthy development of these systems with potentially long-lasting, adverse effects.

Also, because children's systems are immature, their ability to detoxify chemicals is less developed than that of adults. Consequently, when an exposure takes place, the residence time of the chemical may be significantly longer than if the same exposure took place in an adult. Last, children have more future years of life than adults, resulting in more time to develop diseases that are the consequence of early exposures.[1]

All of this underscores that we ought to be vigilant in our efforts to minimize our children's exposure to harmful ingredients in personal care products.

Phthalates were discussed in the introduction to the personal care section (see page 27). They are ubiquitous—found in everything from lotions to toys, cosmetics, and plastic products. "Phthalates are not chemically bound to these products," according to an article in the journal *Pediatrics*, "and are therefore continuously released into the air or through leaching into liquids, leading to exposure through ingestion, dermal transfer, and inhalation"[2] As noted in the previous section, among the concerns about the use of products containing phthalates is permanent damage to the endocrine and reproductive systems. They are also associated with allergies and are known animal carcinogens.

A recent study in the journal *Pediatrics* found that reported use of lotion, shampoo, and baby powder was associated with higher concentrations of urinary phthalates. It was concluded that absorption through the skin was likely a significant contributor to the increased urinary phthalate levels found in the study subjects. In 2006, the European Union banned the use of six different phthalates because of the concerns over the toxicity of these chemicals to young children; in the United States, however, there is no similar ban, nor is there a requirement to label products according to their phthalate content. This makes it difficult for parents to make informed decisions about the products they bring into their homes and use on their children.

Although the phthalate issue is only one of many when it comes to potentially harmful ingredients in personal care products, it is representative of the myriad concerns about many products marketed for children.

An industry-funded body, the Cosmetic Ingredient Review, checks in to the safety of cosmetics ingredients. However, according to the Environmental Working Group, the Cosmetics Ingredient Review has not tested the safety of 77 percent of the ingredients in children's products now on the market.[3] That means one thing for child consumers: They are guinea pigs—subjects in an uncontrolled experiment.

The Environmental Working Group compiled the *Parent's Buying Guide*, which is a safety guide for children's personal care products. The products recommended in this chapter have been derived from it. I encourage you to read through the guide and review the comprehensive list of safer product picks.

The Case for Safe Soap and Body Wash

Some soap and body wash products contain phthalates. Often you will find phthalates disguised on product labels by the word *fragrance*. Phthalate exposure in children has been linked to eczema, allergies, disruptions in the normal function of their hormones, and male genital development issues. Other chemicals to avoid in soap are triclosan, found in many antibacterial soap products, and DMDM hydantoin.

Parabens are another controversial class of chemicals. These are widely used as preservatives. They are known hormone disruptors—that is, they interfere with the normal functioning of the endocrine system. (The endocrine system produces and secretes hormones that regulate the body's growth, metabolism, and sexual development.) There is debate within the scientific community about whether or not parabens are carcinogens.

Recommended safer soap and body wash brands are below. These recommendations are from the Environmental Working Group's Cosmetics Database (www.cosmeticsdatabase.com).

- ☼ Aubrey Organics
- ☼ Avalon Organics
- ☼ Burt's Bees
- ☼ California Baby
- ☼ Earth Tribe
- ☼ Peter Rabbit Organics
- ☼ Tom's of Maine

The Case for Safe Shampoo and Conditioner

Many conventional shampoo and conditioner products for children contain fragrance (phthalates) and preservatives (parabens). It is not unusual for the fragrance and preservatives to include chemicals that are known carcinogens, neurotoxins, and endocrine disruptors. There is also evidence indicating that sodium lauryl sulfate (SLS) and sodium laureth sulfate (SLES) are linked with eye and immune system damage, among other issues.

Recommended safer shampoo and conditioner brands are below. These recommendations are from the Environmental Working Group's Cosmetics Database (www.cosmeticsdatabase.com).

- ✿ Aubrey Organics
- ✿ Avalon Organics
- ✿ Burt's Bees
- ✿ California Baby
- ✿ Dr. Bronner's
- ✿ Peter Rabbit Organics

The Case for Safe Body Lotion

One of the important differences between children's skin and adult skin is that it is thinner and therefore absorbs more of what is put directly on it. Potentially harmful ingredients found in some lotion products are parabens (preservatives), phthalates, and PEG (polyethylene glycol) compounds. Exposure to PEG compounds have been linked to several types of cancer.

The list below identifies some of the safer brands of lotions for children. These recommendations are from the Environmental Working Group's Cosmetics Database (www.cosmeticsdatabase.com).

- ✿ Aubrey Organics
- ✿ Avalon Organics
- ✿ California Baby
- ✿ Dancing Dingo
- ✿ Vaseline Petroleum Jelly

The Case for Safe Sunscreen

Recently the Environmental Working Group published a study on sunscreen product safety and effectiveness. The findings were interesting in that many products contained ingredients linked to cancer-causing chemicals, and most products did not effectively protect people from the sun's harmful UVA radiation! The authors of the study reported that many of the sunscreen market leaders' products did not meet the Environmental Working Group's criteria for safety and effectiveness.[4]

Generally speaking, products that are not absorbed into the skin, but rather reflect the sun's rays, are recommended. These products contain zinc and titanium oxide.

Recommended safer sunscreen brands for your children are below. These recommendations are from the Environmental Working Group's Cosmetics Database (www.cosmeticsdatabase.com). *Note:* Experts do not recommend using sunscreen products on babies younger than six months old.

Table 7.1 Safe Sunscreen Products

BRAND	NOTES
Blue Lizard	
California Baby	No fragrance; SPF 30+
CVS	With zinc oxide
Jason Natural Cosmetics	
Kiss My Face	Paraben-free
Mustela	SPF 50
Olay	Defense Daily UV Moisturizer (with zinc)
Walgreens	(Only its product with zinc oxide)

The Case for Safe Toothpaste

The American Dental Association recommends that children under the age of two use toothpaste that is fluoride-free, and the Centers for Disease Control and Prevention recommends that children under the age of six use toothpaste that has a reduced amount of fluoride relative to that found in regular toothpaste for adults.

Fluoride, if ingested in large enough doses, can discolor teeth and can even be poisonous. Other ingredients the Environmental Working Group recommends against are triclosan and PEG compounds.

Triclosan is an antimicrobial and antifungal pesticide. Its adverse effects on human health and the environment are well documented and include allergic reactions and skin irritation. Exposure to triclosan can contribute to antibiotic resistance and has been linked to liver and inhalation toxicity. Low-level exposure may disrupt the normal function of the thyroid hormone system (normal functioning of this particular hormone is key to brain growth and development in fetuses). If that isn't enough, triclosan degrades into dioxins and chlorophenols, both of which are known carcinogens. This stuff not only poses a threat to human health, but when it breaks down into cancer-causing agents, it also wreaks havoc with animals in our ecosystem.

Below is a list of safe toothpaste brands.

- ✿ Burt's Bees
- ✿ Desert Essence
- ✿ Jason Natural Cosmetics
- ✿ Nature's Gate
- ✿ Peelu
- ✿ Tom's of Maine
- ✿ Weleda

The Case for Safe Baby Wipes

There are a few ingredients that would be wise to avoid when selecting baby wipes. Fragrance is at the top of the list, as exposure to some ingredients in "fragrance" cocktails has been shown to cause immune system damage, along with damage to the brain and nervous system. DMDM hydantoin is another product to keep away from in baby wipes: It has been linked to immune system damage; irritation of the skin, eyes, and lungs; and organ system toxicity. The third ingredient to watch out for when buying baby wipes is 2-bromo 2-nitropropane-1, 3-diol. This is another irritant that can form into carcinogens. Currently the list is not long for safer baby wipe options, but that's sure to change over time. For updates, check the Environmental Working Group site (see Resources section on page 107).

Following is the short list of recommended baby wipe brands.

- ☼ Avalon Organics
- ☼ Pampers (unscented only)
- ☼ Seventh Generation
- ☼ Tushies

It's easy and economical to make your own baby wipes, using paper towels and a mixture of water, olive oil, and baby shampoo. Soak a three-inch-high stack of paper towels in a mixture of 1 cup of warm water and 1 teaspoon each of olive oil and baby shampoo, and voilà. (Adjust the amount of water, oil, and shampoo according to the number of paper towels used.) Store in a recycled plastic baby wipes container or a plastic resealable bag.

The Case for Safe Diaper Cream

When choosing a diaper cream, look for one that is free of butylated hydroxyanisole (BHA) and fragrance. BHA has a long list of both proven and possible human health concerns, and is a banned substance for products sold in the European Union. Fragrance, too, is associated with a range of health hazards from allergies to hormone system disruption. Following is a list of safe diaper creams.

- ✿ Aquaphor
- ✿ Balmex
- ✿ Burt's Bees
- ✿ Triple Paste Medicated Ointment
- ✿ Weleda

The Case for Skipping Baby Powder

The experts say that it's best not to use baby powder altogether, due to the damage the tiny powder particles can cause to a baby's lungs. Talc, a mineral found in talcum powder, is a close cousin of the very dangerous mineral asbestos. When inhaled, talc can lead to respiratory issues such as pneumonia and lung irritation.[5] If baby powder is used, avoid powder with fragrance, sodium borate, or DMDM hydantoin.

CHAPTER 8

Hair Care

Most women (and many men!) care about the way their hair looks, and are somewhat particular about the products they use. Finding shampoo and conditioners that are plant-based and void of harmful chemicals and do a decent job cleaning and conditioning your hair is possible!

There are a number of products you can find at natural food stores and, increasingly, on your supermarket's shelves. In fact, even Wal-Mart now carries some of the safer brands in its Organic Beauty section. The scenario changes, however, if you're looking for styling and coloring products that both work and are free of suspect ingredients. As things stand in early 2009, the marketplace has relatively few safe styling and coloring options available.

The Case for Safe Shampoo and Conditioner

The primary reason to be choosy when it comes to your family's daily hair care products is ingredients such as sodium lauryl sulfate (SLS), sodium laureth sulfate (SLES), fragrance, and parabens. SLS and SLES are in the majority of conventional shampoos, and although there continues to be some controversy over the impact of these foaming agents, studies have linked them to eye, organ, and immune system damage. SLES is frequently contaminated with dioxane, a probable human carcinogen according to the Environmental Protection Agency.[1]

Fragrance and parabens are proven carcinogens and neurotoxins and have been shown to interfere with the normal function of the endocrine system. There are numerous other ingredients in shampoos and conditioners that have been linked to adverse health effects. Safer brands are in the following list.

- ✿ Alba
- ✿ Aubrey Organics
- ✿ Avalon Organics
- ✿ Aveda
- ✿ Belegenza
- ✿ Burt's Bees
- ✿ Collective Wellbeing
- ✿ Desert Essences
- ✿ Dr. Hauschka
- ✿ Druide

- ✿ Eco Bella
- ✿ Giovanni
- ✿ Hamadi
- ✿ John Masters Organics
- ✿ Jurlique
- ✿ Nature Girl
- ✿ Ole Henriksen
- ✿ Red Flower
- ✿ Suki
- ✿ Surya
- ✿ Weleda

If you are looking for dandruff shampoo, you should know that conventional dandruff shampoos contain coal tar, which is a dangerous carcinogen. SLS and SLES are both skin irritants, and can lead to a flaky, itchy scalp, so it makes sense to first ensure that the shampoo you are using does not have either ingredient. Natural remedies for a flaky scalp are rose-mary and tea tree oil. Consider adding a few drops of the essential oil of either to a small amount of a safer shampoo.[2]

The Case for Safer Hair Dye

Did you know that over 60 percent of women use some type of hair dye? There have been a handful of studies done on the use of hair dye and its impact on human health. The chemicals in hair dye, particularly darker shades, have been demonstrated to be carcinogenic, and some links have been drawn between hair dye exposure and bladder cancer, lymphoma, and leukemia. Most studies correlate the length of time a person uses hair dye with increased risk of disease.

A study published in the *American Journal of Epidemiology* in the spring of 2008 reports that women (not men) who use hair dye have an increased risk of the blood cancer non-Hodgkin's lymphoma.[3] The study is one of the most comprehensive conducted to date and aimed to clarify inconsistent/inconclusive results reported from previous studies. It concludes that the risk is greatest for women who started using hair dye before 1980; for women who have been consistently using hair dye after 1980, the risk was limited to those who used a dark dye. (Some of the coloring agents proved to be carcinogenic in rodents in studies conducted in the 1970s were removed from hair dyes by 1980.) Another study, also published in the spring of 2008, in *The Lancet Oncology,* noted that there is also likely an increased risk of bladder cancer for hairdressers and barbers who use dyes on their clients.[4]

A further indication that traditional hair dyes ought to be removed from your beauty regimen is that the European Union enacted a ban in December 2006 for twenty-two chemicals that appear in hair dye that have never been tested for safety in humans. The European commission responsible for the directive cited correlations to bladder cancer as the primary health concern. The studies cited above along with the chemical ban in the European Union point to the fact that it would be smart to forgo conventional hair dye products, particularly if you use a darker shade.

There are some natural, plant-based dyes on the market, most of which use henna in combination with other plant-based dyes.

There are two categories of dye that are safer than the traditional products. The "safer" category is not altogether devoid of dangerous chemicals (particularly one called p-phenylenediamine), but the chemicals of concern exist in very low levels.[5] You'll find these options in the following list.

- ✿ Eco Colors
- ✿ Henna Company
- ✿ Herbavita
- ✿ Naturcolor
- ✿ Tints of Nature

There is an even smaller category of nontoxic hair color products:

- ✿ Igora Botanic
- ✿ Light Mountain
- ✿ Logona

The Case for Safer Hair-Styling Products

Many hair-styling products contain synthetic fragrance, parabens, ureas, 1,4 dioxane (often appearing on labels as PEG), and various ammonia compounds. Fragrance, which sounds like only one ingredient, is actually a cocktail of numerous ingredients, some of which are phthalates. Phthalates are endocrine disruptors, and recent studies have shown that low-dose exposure to some phthalates can impair normal genital development in males in utero.[6] Other studies link higher-dose exposures to adult infertility.

Parabens, as discussed in previous sections, have been shown to interfere with the normal functioning of the hormone system. Ureas (diazolidinyl urea, imidazolidinyl urea, DMDM hydantoin, and sodium hydroxymethylglycinate) can cause skin rashes and irritation, and 1,4 dioxane is a carcinogen. The number of harmful or suspected harmful ingredients does not stop there. Suffice it to say that most hairstyling products are full of ingredients that are best not used if you want to protect your health.

Safer brand alternatives to many of the conventional products are listed below.

- ✿ Aubrey Organics
- ✿ Aveda
- ✿ Belegenza
- ✿ Burt's Bees
- ✿ Collective Wellbeing
- ✿ Druide
- ✿ Giovanni Organic Hair Care
- ✿ Hamadi
- ✿ John Masters Organics
- ✿ Jurlique
- ✿ Miessence
- ✿ Modern Organic Products

CHAPTER 9

Skin Care

The Case for Safe Soap

Many soaps on the market today are made with ingredients that pose potential health risks to those who use them. Antimicrobial soaps contain a host of ingredients that are best avoided, including methylisothiazolinone (MIT) and triclosan. MIT has been shown to cause nervous system damage and exposure has been linked to Alzheimer's disease. Triclosan is classified as a pesticide by the Environmental Protection Agency; it seems ridiculous to assume that we can effectively and safely clean our bodies with a chemical developed to kill pests! In addition, sunlight can convert this ingredient into dioxin, which is an extremely potent carcinogen.[1]

The endocrine system regulates the production of hormones. Additives designed to make many soaps smell good (often appearing as the word *fragrance* on the label) are linked to endocrine system damage.

Following are safe body soap brands.

- ✿ Alba
- ✿ Aubrey Organics
- ✿ Avalon Organics
- ✿ Burt's Bees
- ✿ Dr. Bronner's
- ✿ Dr. Hauschka
- ✿ Druide
- ✿ Ecco Bella
- ✿ Kiss My Face
- ✿ John Masters Organics
- ✿ Juice Beauty
- ✿ Pangea Organics
- ✿ Tom's of Maine
- ✿ Weleda
- ✿ Whole Foods brand soaps

The Case for Safe Body and Face Lotion

The primary ingredients in conventional lotion that are cause for concern are fragrance and preservatives. Fragrance contains phthalates, which are those hormone-mimicking chemicals that can lead to genital development defects in unborn children. Synthetic preservatives such as parabens are implicated in reproductive damage and birth defects; parabens have also been linked to both breast and prostate cancer.[2]

Many companies committed to producing natural body lotion products use essential oils to make their products smell nice, and they use natural preservatives. A rule of thumb to keep in mind is that you should be able to pronounce all of the ingredients listed on a lotion bottle or tube! There are a number of excellent, all-natural lotions available. Keeping in mind that lotion is applied to the skin and designed to be absorbed by it, it seems wise to be careful when choosing these products.

The following companies are recommended for safe lotions.

- Alba
- Annemarie Borlind
- Astara Biogenic Skincare
- Aubrey Organics
- Avalon Organics
- Burt's Bees
- Dr. Hauschka
- Druide
- Ecco Bella
- Éminence Organics
- Garden of Eve
- Healing-scents
- John Masters Organics
- Juice Beauty
- Jurlique
- Kimberly Sayer of London
- Kiss My Face
- Korres Natural Products
- Mychelle Dermaceuticals

- ✿ Nature Girl
- ✿ Ole Henriksen
- ✿ Pangea Organics
- ✿ Poofy Organics
- ✿ Shikai Borage
- ✿ Suki
- ✿ Weleda

The Case for Safe Antiperspirant / Deodorant

The story with some brands of antiperspirant and deodorant is not too different from that of many other personal care products: Look out for parabens and phthalates. Parabens are commonly used preservative agents that are known hormone disruptors and have been linked to breast cancer.[3] Phthalates are used to help our personal care products smell nice, but their contents can make us sick. They contain ingredients known to disrupt the normal functioning of the endocrine system, and many fragrances contain volatile organic compounds (VOCs), which can include dangerous carcinogens, such as formaldehyde.

You may have heard or read about the possible link between Alzheimer's and aluminum compounds found in many deodorants/antiperspirants. Aluminum is a strong astringent and closes the body's pores, preventing sweat and odor from escaping. The ingredient works well in terms of preventing sweat and odor;

however, it has been the subject of debate in terms of its potential health risks. Alzheimer's patients tend to have elevated levels of aluminum in their brain (which is where heavy metals are shown to accumulate). While the jury is still considered out with respect to this association, aluminum is a known neurotoxin, and for this reason alone it may be best to opt for a less risky choice when it comes to deodorant.

Who knew that our armpits could be the source of such contention! No one I know is a fan of body odor, but it is a fact of life for some of us, and can occur when odor-causing bacteria develop in our underarms.

In conducting research for this book, I tried a number of the brands listed below. Some worked better than others, and it is my guess that most people will need to experiment a bit given the differences in our body chemistry. Look for a phthalate-free label on your deodorant; select one that incorporates essential oils for its fragrance.

- Alba
- Almay
- Aubrey Organics
- Avalon Organics
- Ban (unscented)
- Burt's Bees
- Crystal
- Desert Essence
- Dr. Hauschka
- Jason

☞ Kiss My Face
☞ Nature's Gate
☞ Speed Stick, unscented
☞ Terressentials
☞ Tom's of Maine
☞ Weleda

The Case for Safe Shaving Cream

Many shaving cream products contain triethanolamine (TEA), a derivative of ammonia and one of the most prevalent and harmful chemicals added to personal care products. In the late 1990s, the National Toxicology program declared it a carcinogen. TEA is also a hormone disruptor. Another ingredient commonly found in shaving cream products is fragrance, which includes more hormone-disrupting chemicals—phthalates. In addition, you'll often find parabens, used as a preservative but which are also hormone disruptors.

When choosing a shaving cream, look for one that is plant-based and uses essential oils for fragrance. Following are safe shaving cream brands.

☞ Aubrey Organics
☞ Avalon Organics
☞ Dr. Bronner's
☞ Kiss my Face
☞ Miessence
☞ Poofy Organics
☞ The Art of Shaving

The Case for Safe Sunscreens

The Environmental Working Group (EWG) recently conducted an in-depth analysis of over a thousand sunscreen products. Its findings were sobering: Four out of five products either didn't provide adequate protection from the sun or contained ingredients for which there are serious safety concerns.

In short, when making sunscreen product choices, the EWG recommends steering clear of oxybenzone, or benzophenone-3, as this ingredient has been linked with skin allergies and endocrine system disruption. It is also recommended that spray sunscreens be avoided because of the risk of inhaling the product. Skipping over sunscreens with fragrance listed as an ingredient is also wise, because of potential reproductive health issues associated with fragrance concoctions.

What should you look for? You want a sunscreen with at least 30 SPF protection, that blocks UVA and UVB rays, and that contains at least 7 percent zinc oxide or titanium oxide. You can read more about the Environmental Working Group's study by visiting the Cosmetics Database Web site (www.cosmeticsdatabase.com) and entering "sunscreen study" into the site's search box. The top ten sunscreen products as recommended by the EWG are listed in the table below.

Table 9.1 Safe Sunscreen Products

BRAND	NOTES
Blue Lizard	Anything without oxybenzone
California Baby	Anything with an SPF of 30 & higher
CVS with zinc oxide	
Jason Natural Cosmetics Sunbrellas Mineral Based Sunblock	
Kiss My Face	"Paraben-free" series
Neutrogena Sensitive Skin Sunblock	
Olay Defense Daily UV Moisturizer	With zinc
SkinCeuticals Physical UV Defense	
Solar Sense Clear Zinc for Face	

The Case for Safe Insect Repellents

There are certainly some compelling reasons to use insect repellant. For example, Lyme disease and the West Nile virus have received a lot of attention in recent years. Lyme disease is transmitted by the deer tick, and is common in some parts of North America, particularly in New England and the Mid-Atlantic and the East–North Central regions. The West Nile virus is a potentially serious illness that is transmitted by mosquitoes. The risk of contracting either Lyme disease or the West Nile virus can be decreased through the use of insect repellents.

There are a host of effective products available, but some contain ingredients that pose risks to human health. The chemical DEET is an ingredient commonly found in insect repellents. Exposure to DEET can result in skin irritation, dizziness, or seizures, and can have other adverse neurological effects. Many insect repellents also contain phthalates. Phthalate exposure has been shown to have adverse effects on the male reproductive system, among other serious health concerns.

When selecting an insect repellent, look for a product that uses picaridin, or oil of lemon eucalyptus. Following is a list of safe insect-repellent brands.

- Bug Off!
- Burt's Bees
- Buzz Away
- Caribbean Blue
- Kiss My Face
- Jason
- Natrapel

CHAPTER 10
Oral Care

The Case for Safe Toothpaste

Some brands of toothpaste contain a wide array of chemicals that have been linked to negative health effects. Triclosan, an antibacterial agent, is a known hormone disruptor. Other hormone disruptors found in some toothpastes are the preservative agents parabens, which can mimic estrogen in the body and lead to an increased chance of breast cancer.

Other ingredients commonly found in toothpaste are sodium lauryl sulfate, or SLS, a foaming agent and suspected carcinogen, and several artificial FD&C (food, drug, and cosmetic) dyes. FD&C Blue 1, Green 3, and Yellow 5 and 6 have all demonstrated some carcinogenic properties. Toothpaste brands that do not use ingredients implicated in adverse health effects are listed atop the following page.

- ✿ Burt's Bees
- ✿ Desert Essence Toothpaste
- ✿ Healing-Scents Toothpaste
- ✿ Jason Natural Toothpaste
- ✿ Kiss My Face Toothpaste
- ✿ Miessence Toothpaste
- ✿ Nature's Gate
- ✿ Peelu
- ✿ Tom's of Maine
- ✿ Weleda

The Case for Safe Mouthwash

Conventional mouthwash products contain a number of ingredients that are potentially dangerous to human health. Alcohol is at the top of the list, as it comprises a large percentage of mouthwash. It is typically found in mouthwash products that are highly acidic; these products can lead to tooth enamel loss and tooth sensitivity.[1] You will also find synthetic dyes and sweeteners, both of which are possible carcinogens. Several of the FD&C dyes are coal-based and have a sketchy regulatory history, indicative of their potential for adverse health effects.

Following are safer mouthwash brands.

- ✿ Aubrey Organics
- ✿ Eco-DenT
- ✿ Healing-Scents
- ✿ Jason
- ✿ Miessence
- ✿ Tom's of Maine
- ✿ Weleda

CHAPTER 11

Cosmetics

Cosmetics have been used almost as long as humans have been wandering the earth. In fact, some of the cosmetics we use today have something in common with those used by ancient Romans in 4000 BCE. Thousands of years ago, they used ingredients such as lead and mercury on their faces; many of us are unwittingly using lead on our lips when we put on lipstick.

The Case for Safe Cosmetics

Only within the last decade has the spotlight shone brightly on the suspect ingredients in many cosmetic products. In the year 2000, the Environmental Working Group published a report about the high levels of phthalates found in nail polish. In the same year, the Centers for Disease Control and Prevention released a report confirming that the highest levels of phthalates are found among women of childbearing age. These reports fueled the fire to address not only the phthalate issue, but also the numerous other potentially harmful ingredients found in many conventional cosmetic products sold in the United States.

The Campaign for Safe Cosmetics grew out of these initial efforts and the increasing concern over dangerous chemicals in cosmetics. There was a noticeable absence of regulation to protect consumers. The Campaign for Safe Cosmetics is a U.S.-based coalition of nonprofit health and environmental organizations that formed in 2004; its mission is to protect the health of consumers by applying pressure to the personal care industry to replace with safer alternatives the ingredients that pose risks to human health.

Through the efforts of the Campaign for Safe Cosmetics, more than a thousand companies have signed the Compact for Safe Cosmetics, which is a pledge to remove harmful ingredients from cosmetics. For additional information and to see a list of the signers, visit www.safecosmetics.org.

One important thing to keep in mind when making cosmetic purchases is that most cosmetics are applied to our faces, where our skin is more delicate and generally thinner than on other parts of the body. Remember that our skin absorbs up to 60 percent of what is applied to it.

The usual suspects are found in many conventional cosmetics—parabens used to preserve the shelf life of products and phthalates to make them smell pleasant. In addition to those two groups of synthetic chemicals, you'll find colorants and dyes.

Safe Cosmetic Brands are listed below. These products can often be found at the local health food market, online, and increasingly at retailers such as Target and Wal-Mart.

- Annemarie Borlind
- Aubrey Organics
- Aveda
- Burt's Bees
- Cleure Cosmetics
- Coastal Classic Creations
- Dr. Hauschka
- Ecco Bella
- Everlast Beauty Silk and Pearl Makeup
- Gourmet Body Treats
- Kiss My Face
- Korres
- Larénim
- Miessence
- Mineral Fusion Cosmetics
- NVEY
- Rejuva Minerals
- RMS Beauty
- Terra Firma
- Zosimos Botanicals

Some nail polish brands harbor some particularly nasty chemicals, including toluene, formaldehyde, and dibutyl phthalate (DPB). These chemicals have been linked in numerous studies with birth defects and cancer.[1] Following are safe nail polish brands.

- ☼ Honey Bee Gardens
- ☼ Nicole by Opi
- ☼ No Miss
- ☼ PeaceKeeper Cause-Metics
- ☼ Priti
- ☼ Sally Hansen
- ☼ SpaRitual
- ☼ Zoya

Green Cleaning

Cleaning, to some degree, is a fact of life. The place we call home needs cleaning on a somewhat regular basis, which necessitates purchasing products that do the job. So what is green cleaning and why should we care about it, particularly in the face of what seem like daunting environmental issues such as climate change and a diminishing global supply of fresh water?

Green cleaning means cleaning to protect health without harming the environment. And we should care about it because many conventional cleaning products pollute the air in our homes, and contain chemicals linked to adverse health effects.

There are roughly 80,000 chemicals used in commerce today. Of those, only 2 percent have been tested and found to be safe for human exposure. To put it another way, 78,000 synthetic chemicals have not been tested for safety. (Also worth noting is that most exposure standards are based on a 180-pound male.) The fact that only 2 percent of the chemicals used in commerce today have been tested for safety does not mean that all of those untested chemicals, were we to be exposed to them, would be catalysts for irregular cell division; it does mean, though, that we are rolling the dice when we use these products.

The negative impact of many conventional cleaning products isn't limited to exposure to them in the home. Workers are exposed when the products are manufactured, and the environment can be damaged from the waste created during production. Then, there is some chemical exposure when the product is being used in the home, as well as environmental damage if a product works its way into the wastewater system. And when you are finished using the product, the residual chemicals can leach into the environment through the landfill.

Small, relatively painless changes in your cleaning routine can yield big dividends for the health of your family.

CHAPTER 12

Indoor Air Quality

One thing we know for sure is that using conventional cleaning products diminishes the quality of the air in our homes. Numerous air-quality studies have confirmed that indoor air quality is two to five times worse than the quality of the air outdoors.[1] You may have heard of sick building syndrome; this condition is caused by inadequate ventilation, chemical contaminants, biological contaminants, or some combination of the three. Symptoms include headache; dry eyes, nose, and mouth; dry skin; and difficulty concentrating. Our health is negatively impacted when we breathe in chemically infused air.

One of the best ways to improve the quality of the air in our home is through the use of houseplants. In the late 1980s, NASA conducted a two-year study examining the impact of houseplants on indoor air quality. It tested for several chemicals commonly found in indoor spaces, such as trichloroethylene, benzene, and formaldehyde. The results were interesting, in that all plants tested yielded some improvement in air quality, but some species were excellent at absorbing specific chemicals. For example, golden pothos and spider plants were best for removing formaldehyde from the air. Formaldehyde is found in natural gases used in cooking and heating, and it's found in many building and cleaning materials. The chart below lists the plants tested by NASA, their light requirements and the chemical(s) they demonstrated an ability to absorb well.

Table 12.1 Houseplants Known to Improve Indoor Air Quality

PLANT	LIGHT REQUIREMENT	GOOD AT REMOVING FROM AIR
Areca palm	Bright	
Bamboo palm	Low to medium	Benzene, trichloroethylene
Boston fern	Medium	
Chinese evergreen	Low to medium	
Chrysanthemum	Bright	Benzene, trichloroethylene
Dracaena	Low to medium	
English ivy	Medium	Benzene
Gerbera daisy	Bright	Benzene, trichloroethylene
Peace lily	Low to medium	Benzene
Rubber tree (*Ficus elastica*)	Medium	
Philodendron	Low to medium	Formaldehyde

PLANT	LIGHT REQUIREMENT	GOOD AT REMOVING FROM AIR
Pothos (golden)	Low to medium	Formaldehyde
Snake plant	Low to medium	Benzene
Spider plant	Low to medium	Formaldehyde
Weeping fig (*Ficus benjamina*)	Medium	Formaldehyde

For a 2,000-square-foot home, fifteen plants, grown in at least six-inch containers, should be present to yield a detectable improvement in air quality.

With a combination of houseplants placed in various rooms throughout the home and the use of some of the recommended green cleaning products found on the following pages, you will be well on your way to protecting your family's health and improving the air quality in your home.

CHAPTER 13

The Kitchen

The kitchen just might be the busiest room in the house, particularly if children are around. Consequently, the kitchen requires some degree of daily cleaning. This chapter provides information about safe products for the various cleaning-related tasks in the kitchen.

The Case for Safe All-Purpose Cleaners

As stated earlier, many conventional cleaning agents contain chemicals that are unsafe for human exposure. Routes of exposure for these chemicals to enter the body include inhalation, ingestion, and contact through the skin or eyes. There are acute or short-term impacts of exposure as well as long-term impacts.

Typically, the short-term impacts from exposure to some conventional all-purpose cleaners are things many of us have experienced at one time or another, such as eye and skin irritation, dizziness, and nausea. Ammonia, chlorine, and glycol ether are some of the chemicals that cause these common side effects.[1]

Long-term, or chronic, exposure often results in damage to organs, such as the kidney and the liver. Glycol ether and diethanolamine (DEA) are both found in some all-purpose cleaners that have been reported to cause organ damage.[2]

Understanding the impact of chemical exposure that accumulates in our bodies over time is complex. Most of us have varying exposure thresholds before things inside begin to go haywire, making it difficult to pinpoint just how much exposure is too much. That being said, the conservative approach is to minimize exposure to the extent possible.

The products listed below are free of synthetic chemicals linked to health problems. If you opt for a brand not listed here, look for biodegradable products that are plant-based and free of dyes and synthetic fragrance. The products should also contain no ammonia and no chlorine.

Table 13.1 Safe All-Purpose Cleaners

BRAND	PRODUCT NAME
Biokleen	Super Concentrated All Purpose Cleaner & Degreaser
Bon Ami	Cleaning Powder
Citra-solv	Concentrate or Ready-to-Use

BRAND	PRODUCT NAME
Earth Friendly Products	Parsley Plus All Purpose Kleener
Ecover	All Purpose Cleaner
Method	All Purpose Cleaner
Mrs. Meyer's Clean Day	All Purpose Cleaner
Planet	All Purpose Spray Cleaner
Seventh Generation	Natural All Purpose Cleaner
Shaklee	Basic H^2 Organic Super Cleaning Concentrate

The Case for Safe Liquid Dish Soap

Many conventional liquid dish soaps contain artificial colors and fragrance. Synthetic fragrance is often petroleum-based, which puts it squarely into the category of a nonrenewable resource. In addition, the chemicals in various fragrance concoctions have been identified as hormone disruptors. (Hormone disruptors are synthetic chemicals that interfere with the normal production of hormones.) Studies have demonstrated that exposure to hormone disruptors can increase the chance of birth defects, particularly in boys, may lead to the early onset of puberty, and cause neural damage. Who wants to expose his or her little ones to this array of nasty stuff?

Many conventional liquid dish soaps also contain surfactants. Surfactants are designed to reduce the surface tension of water, enabling water to quickly coat the surface being cleaned and to get underneath dirt and debris so that they can be easily removed. Although surfactants haven't been linked to harmful impacts on human health, certain types of surfactants are highly processed, slow to biodegrade, and tough on marine life.

Table 13.2 Safe Liquid Dish Soap Products

BRAND	PRODUCT NAME
Biokleen	Hand Moisturizing Dishwash Liquid
Citra-solv	Citra Dish Natural Liquid Dish Soap
Earth Friendly Products	Dishmate
Ecover	Dishwashing Liquid
Method	Dish Soap
Mrs. Meyer's Clean Day	Dish Soap
Planet	Ultra Dishwashing Liquid
Seventh Generation	Natural Dish Liquid
Shaklee	Dish Wash Concentrate

The Case for Safe Automatic Dishwasher Soap

There are a few bad boys in many conventional automatic dishwasher soaps. The ingredient at the top of the list is chlorine bleach. Chlorine is extremely damaging to the human body. When mixed with heated dishwasher water, chlorine can leach into the air in your kitchen, making it unsafe to breathe. Also, trace amounts of residual chlorine might linger on your dishes. How do you like the irony! Dish detergent lacing dishes with nasty chemicals that are unsafe for humans to ingest!

Some conventional automatic dish soaps contain phosphates. Like some surfactants, phosphates are not known to pose threats to human health; however, they do pose a threat to the environment. When phosphates wind up in waterways, like rivers, they can fertilize algal populations, leading to large algal blooms that in turn choke out plant and animal life in aquatic ecosystems. This is called *eutrification*, and along with agricultural runoff contributes to aquatic dead zones.

Table 13.3 Safe Automatic Dishwasher Detergent Products

BRAND	PRODUCT NAME
Biokleen	Automatic Dish Powder
Citra-solv	Citra Dish (powder or liquid)
Earth Friendly Products	Wave (powder, gel, or tablets)
Ecover	Automatic Dishwashing Powder
Method	Smarty Dish
Mrs. Meyer's Clean Day	Automatic Dishwashing Liquid or Dish Packs
Planet	Automatic Dishwasher Detergent
Seventh Generation	Automatic Dishwasher (detergent pacs or gel)
Shaklee	Dish Wash Automatic Concentrate

The Case for Safe Glass and Mirror Cleaners

Are you driven crazy by smudges on the microwave or fingerprints on a glass door? Remember that cleaning glass and mirrors usually involves a spray bottle, which releases hundreds of tiny droplets of the cleaner into the air. We then lean into the space we have just sprayed, breathing the air and the glass cleaner as we clean.

Many traditional glass cleaners contain ammonia, butyl cellulose, and naphtha (petroleum distillates). Ammonia is a severe respiratory-tract irritant and can be an eye and nose irritant. Butyl cellulose and naphtha are skin and lung irritants, and long-term exposure has been linked to organ damage.

Table 13.4 Safe Glass and Mirror Products

BRAND	PRODUCT NAME
Biokleen	Ammonia Free Glass Cleaner
Citra-solv	Citra Clear Natural Window & Glass Cleaner
Earth Friendly Products	Window Kleener
Ecover	Glass & Surface Cleaner
Method	Best in Glass
Mrs. Meyer's Clean Day	Window Spray
Seventh Generation	Natural Glass & Surface Cleaner

The Case for Safe Floor Cleaners

Warning labels on household cleaning products refer to issues associated with ingestion. Only 10 percent of health problems related to cleaning products used in the home, however, are due to ingestion. A whopping 90 percent of cleaning agent-related health problems is from inhaling the vapors and absorbing the particles of a cleaning agent.

Most conventional floor cleaners contain some of those nasty ingredients that are not safe to inhale, such as ammonia, butyl cellulose, and petroleum distillates.

Table 13.5 Safe Floor Cleaner Products

Brand	Product Name
Biokleen	All Purpose Cleaner
Citra-solv	Natural Cleaner & Degreaser
Earth Friendly Products	Floor Cleaner
Ecover	All Purpose Cleaner
Method	All Floor Cleaner & Good for Wood
Mrs. Meyer's Clean Day	All Purpose Cleaner
Seventh Generation	Natural All Purpose Cleaner

CHAPTER 14

The Bathroom

For me, this room is at the bottom of the list to clean. Bathroom cleaning must be done, however, and given that most bathrooms are not particularly large, it pays to make an effort not to contaminate the air quality with nasty chemicals.

Remember that indoor air quality is on average two to five times worse than is outdoor air quality.[1] Given that, try to open the windows wide, even if it's January and you live in New Hampshire, to circulate that chemical-laced air out and some fresh air in.

The rationale for using safe all-purpose cleaners for the bathroom can be found on page 70–71. Table 14.1 shows recommended all-purpose cleaners.

Table 14.1 Safe All-Purpose Cleaners

BRAND	PRODUCT NAME
Biokleen	Super Concentrated All Purpose Cleaner & Degreaser
Bon Ami	Cleaning Powder
Citra-solv	Concentrate or Ready-to-Use
Earth Friendly Products	Parsley Plus All Purpose Kleener
Ecover	All Purpose Cleaner
Method	All Purpose Cleaner
Mrs. Meyer's Clean Day	All Purpose Cleaner
Planet	All Purpose Spray Cleaner
Seventh Generation	Natural All Purpose Cleaner
Shaklee	Basic H2 Organic Super Cleaning Concentrate

The Case for Safe Tub and Tile Cleaners

Ironically, much of the residue found in most tubs and showers is that left by the various cleaning products we use on ourselves—soap, shampoo, and conditioner, for example. There is also some buildup of deposits left by hard water, and, of course, there's also some good old-fashioned dirt.

Many traditional tub and tile cleaners contain chlorine bleach, hydrochloric and phosphoric acids, and lye (sodium hydroxide).[2] Ammonia is another common ingredient. If these chemicals are inhaled, they can damage lung tissue and cause irritation and breathing difficulty. Tubs and showers are some of the most enclosed spaces in the home, so if toxic chemicals are being used in these confined spaces, you can bet that the air quality in there is terrible, and it's going right into the body of whoever is doing the cleaning. Table 14.2 shows recommended tub and tile cleaners.

Table 14.2 Safe Tub and Tile Cleaners

BRAND	PRODUCT NAME
Bon Ami	Cleaning Powder
Earth Friendly Products	Creamy Cleanser
Earth Friendly Products	Shower Kleener
Ecover	Bathroomcleaner
Ecover	Limescale Remover
Method	Tub 'N Tile
Mrs. Meyer's Clean Day	Shower Cleaner
Seventh Generation	Shower Cleaner
Seventh Generation	Tub & Tile Cleaner

The Case for Safe Toilet Bowl Cleaners

Conventional toilet bowl cleaners contain some of the most harmful chemicals found in cleaning agents. The ingredient list may include chlorine bleach, which can burn the skin, eyes, and respiratory tract. Another common ingredient is ammonia, which is an eye, nose, and lung irritant. Exposure can cause wheezing and difficulty breathing as well as chest pain. Some toilet bowl cleaners contain hydrochloric acid.[3]

Hydrochloric acid has been linked to central nervous system disorders and issues with the blood and heart. Other impacts of exposure to hydrochloric acid are irritation to the nose, eyes, throat, and mucous membranes and liver and kidney damage.[4]

Some bowl cleaners contain sulfuric acid, which also poses some potent health threats if inhaled or touched; it's highly corrosive.[5] Also, if chlorine bleach is mixed with a cleaner containing either sulfuric acid or hydrochloric acid, chlorine gas will result and that by-product is extraordinarily damaging to humans.[6] Yikes. Table 14.3 shows recommended toilet bowl-cleaning products.

Table 14.3 Safe Toilet Bowl Products

BRAND	PRODUCT NAME
Earth Friendly Products	Toilet Kleener
Method	'Lil Bowl Blu
Mrs. Meyer's Clean Day	Toilet Bowl Cleaner
Seventh Generation	Toilet Bowl Cleaner

The Case for Safe Drain Openers

Conventional products used to open drains are full of noxious chemicals that are hard on both humans and the environment. Many drain cleaners contain lye (sodium hydroxide), which can be life-threatening if ingested and can burn the skin if touched.[7]

In any shower or tub, there is going to be hair that does not make it all the way down the drain into the septic system or sewer pipe.

I have some advice, based on trying the gamut of products that are out there to help unclog drains. This includes everything from enzyme-based drain openers to the witches' brew of baking soda, vinegar, and boiling water.

My recommendation to alleviate the problem of a clogged drain is to use the tried, true, cheap, and, yes, gross method involving a wire hanger. Grab a small bucket or maybe two: one for whatever it is that the wire hanger helps to pull out of the drain and the other to catch whatever comes up after seeing what's in the first bucket. It's a nasty job, but it doesn't require any chemically laden liquid!

If you are not up to the wire hanger task, the table below shows products that will help with drain woes.

Table 14.4 Safe Drain Openers

BRAND	PRODUCT NAME
Citra-solv	Citra Drain
Earth Friendly Products	Earth Enzymes

CHAPTER 15

The Laundry

Laundry is a seemingly unending task, one that most of us engage in on a weekly if not daily basis. Given the frequency with which we wash our clothes, there is some irony associated with doing the laundry using conventional detergents. We launder our clothes to make them clean for the next time we wear them, right? Depending on the type of detergent you use, there is a chance that you are unintentionally leaving a "dirty" chemical residue on your "clean" clothing.

The Case for Safe Laundry Detergents

You know the potentially hazardous health effects of conventional toilet bowl cleaners, dishwasher detergents, and all-purpose cleaners? Neither the sketchy ingredients nor the potential for harm to your health is significantly different with conventional laundry soap. Many brands contain a fragrance cocktail, which has the potential to wreak havoc with our endocrine system. This system regulates the production of hormones as well as the growth, development, and maturation processes.[1]

According to the Natural Resources Defense Council, an endocrine disruptor is a synthetic chemical that either mimics or blocks hormones and disrupts the body's normal hormonal function.[2] The chemicals that comprise endocrine disruptors, such as phthalates and bisphenol-A, have not been tested for their safety in conjunction with exposure to humans. Unfortunately, this is the case with 95 percent of the synthetic chemicals that are commercially available in the United States today. Europe is well ahead of the United States and Canada on this curve, as the European Union recently passed legislation requiring tests for the safety of these types of chemicals prior to including them in products that are available commercially.

We are living in an age when we see some of the frightening impacts of exposure to endocrine disruptors. What has been found is that exposure to these "gender-bending" chemicals decreases the production of testosterone and mimics female hormones, such as estrogen. Evidence of exposure to endocrine disruptors is shown by a decrease in the male-to-female birth-rate ratio, early onset of puberty, breast cancer, incompletely descended testicles, and insulin resistance.[3] If we can minimize our exposure to the endocrine disruptor chemicals, we can take a step toward minimizing some of the negative health impacts.

Traditional laundry detergents often contain surfactants. Surfactants are designed to reduce the surface tension of water, enabling water to quickly coat the surface being cleaned and to get underneath dirt and debris so that they can be easily removed. Some petroleum-based surfactants are tough on the environment in the sense that they are slow to degrade, but of greater concern is the fact that the chemical benzene is produced during the manufacturing process of surfactants. Benzene is a known carcinogen and exposure has been linked to leukemia and other blood disorders.[4]

Table 15.1 lists safe laundry detergent products, which can be found at most health food stores and, increasingly, in neighborhood groceries.

Table 15.1 Safe Laundry Detergent Products

BRAND	PRODUCT NAME
Biokleen	Laundry Liquid/ Laundry Powder
Borax	20 Mule Team Borax Powder
Caldrea	Laundry Detergent
Citra Solv	Citra Suds Liquid/Citra Suds Liquid Powder
Earth Friendly Products	Ecos Liquid/Ecos Powder Laundry Detergent

BRAND	PRODUCT NAME
Method	HE Compatible Laundry Detergent/HE Compatible Baby Laundry Detergent
Mrs. Meyer's Clean Day	Baby Blossom Laundry Detergent/Laundry Detergent
Planet	Ultra Laundry Detergent Liquid/ 2X Ultra Laundry Detergent HE/ Ultra Powdered Laundry Detergent
Seventh Generation	Baby Liquid Laundry Detergent/Natural 2X Concentrate Laundry Liquid/ Natural Powdered Laundry/ Delicate Care Laundry Detergent
Shaklee	Fresh Laundry Liquid Concentrate/Fresh Laundry Concentrate Powder

The Case for Safe Bleach Products

The reasons for using an alternative to chlorine bleach are numerous. Chlorine, as mentioned previously, is a dangerous chemical known to be corrosive to our skin and eyes. It's a respiratory irritant, and contains toxins that are linked to reproductive, immune, and neurological system damage. It's also poisonous if ingested.

Oxygen bleach is a good alternative to chlorine bleach. Though I've yet to find a brand that whitens as well as does chlorine bleach, oxygen bleach works adequately, and is nontoxic, biodegradable, and a natural disinfectant.[5] Table 15.2 shows safe bleach alternatives.

Table 15.2 Safe Bleach Products

BRAND	PRODUCT NAME
Biokleen	Oxygen Bleach Plus
Ecover	Non-Chlorine Bleach
Seventh Generation	Free & Clear Chlorine Free Bleach
Shaklee	Nature Bright Laundry Booster and Stain Remover

The Case for Safe Fabric Softeners and Dryer Sheets

There is a laundry list of reasons to avoid conventional dryer sheets and liquid fabric softeners! To begin with, they work by coating the surface of fabrics with a chemical cocktail that contains hazardous ingredients such as synthetic fragrances, ammonium chloride, and chloroform. Some of the common ingredients are known neurotoxins and carcinogens.

Dryer sheets may create synthetic estrogen, which can alter the normal function of the endocrine system; some studies have linked synthetic estrogen to increased risk for breast and testicular cancers. These ingredients are released slowly as we sleep on our sheets, dry ourselves with our towels, and wear our clothes; as they are released, we can absorb and inhale them. In addition, there is evidence that soft-eners increase the flammability of fabrics.

There are many easy-to-find alternatives to the synthetic chemical-laden products for softening clothes and eliminating static cling. Below are some recommended products.

Table 15.3 Safe Fabric Softeners and Dryer Sheets

BRAND	PRODUCT NAME
Caldrea	Fabric Softener/Dryer Sheets
Ecover	Fabric Softener
Method	Fabric Softer/Squeaky Green Dryer Cloths
Mrs. Meyer's Clean Day	Fabric Softener/Dryer Sheets
Seventh Generation	Fabric Softener
Shaklee	Soft Fabric Fragrance Free Dryer Sheets

CHAPTER 16

Brewing Your Own

If you have the interest and the time, it's easy and economical to make your own cleaning products. You just need some basics you likely already have on your pantry shelves.

Here are some ideas for do-it-yourself cleaning products. Vinegar, baking soda, Borax, hydrogen peroxide, castile soap, and essential oils are great at accomplishing most of the cleaning tasks required in a house. More important, they pose no risk to the people using them, nor do they pollute the air with nasty fumes.

In the Kitchen

All-Purpose Cleaners

- ☼ Combine 2 tablespoons of white distilled vinegar and 1 teaspoon of Borax in a 16-ounce spray bottle. Fill with hot water and shake to dissolve the Borax. Add ¼ cup of liquid castile soap and you're good to go. Add a dozen or so drops of essential oil if you want to scent the cleaner.

- ☼ Use straight baking soda or Borax as an all-purpose scouring powder.

- ☼ For acidic stains, pour straight club soda into a spray bottle, then spray on the affected area.

- ☼ White distilled vinegar is an excellent antibacterial and antifungal agent. It combats bacteria and germs. Yes, it stinks a bit initially, but after the vinegar has dried, the smell is gone. This is a great way to disinfect countertops and sinks. Try adding a few drops of an aromatic essential oil to the white vinegar to combat the smell.

- ☼ Replace the cap of a hydrogen peroxide bottle with a spray nozzle and use for general cleaning and stain removal. When attempting to remove a stain, let the hydrogen peroxide sit on the surface for a few minutes before wiping clean.

Stainless-Steel-Appliance Cleaner

✿ Use a rag with olive oil on it for a safe and excellent stainless-steel cleaner.

✿ Mix ½ cup of baking soda with enough liquid dish soap to make a paste. Apply with a sponge, then rinse with warm water.

✿ For light cleaning, spritz with white distilled vinegar, then wipe dry.

Window and Glass Cleaner

✿ Use a lint-free cloth and club soda in a spray bottle to clean windows, mirrors, and other glass.

✿ Mix 2 ounces of water with 10 drops of lavender or lemongrass oil to remove dirt from windows.

✿ Put 2 teaspoons of white distilled vinegar into a quart of warm water, then spray on windows or glass.

Floor Cleaner

✿ Mix 2 gallons of warm water, ½ cup of white distilled vinegar (or lemon juice), and ¼ cup of liquid castile soap in a bucket (any type of floor).

✿ Combine a few drops of liquid dish soap with warm water in a bucket (any type of floor).

✿ Use straight club soda to clean a floor (any type of floor).

✿ For vinyl floors, mix ½ gallon of 3 percent hydrogen peroxide with ½ gallon of water, then mop. There is no need to rinse.

Miscellaneous Tips:

- ✿ Add a cup of distilled white vinegar to the dishwasher once in a while to clean and deodorize it.

- ✿ Put 3 cups of water and ½ cup of distilled white vinegar in your automatic coffeemaker to deodorize and clean it. Run through one cycle, then run through one or two more with tap water only.

- ✿ To polish sterling silver, use a bit of toothpaste (see list on page59) on a rag.

- ✿ Move any cleaners with known harmful chemicals that you need/want to keep into a shed or garage to minimize indoor air pollution.

- ✿ Because shoes track in everything from pesticides to pet feces, use a doormat or have a shoes-off policy in your house.

In the Bathroom

Sink, Tub, and Shower Cleaners

- ✿ To combat mildew, wipe the mildew-prone areas with oil. Mildew won't grow where there is light and low humidity, so run a fan to move the air and dry the bathroom. In addition, squeegee walls or glass in the shower.

- ✿ Combine baking soda and castile or liquid soap to form a frostinglike consistency to use as a soft scrub cleanser instead of a sink, tub, and tile cleaner.

- ✿ White distilled vinegar is an excellent

antibacterial and antifungal agent. Spray it on mold-prone areas.

✿ Mix ½ cup of vinegar and 3 tablespoons of salt to remove spots around drains. Apply to affected area and let sit for a little while before rinsing.

✿ To remove soap scum in the shower, spray liberally with a layer of hydrogen peroxide, then a layer of vinegar, then scrub.

Toilet Cleaners

✿ Use ½ cup of baking soda and ½ cup of distilled white vinegar to clean your toilet. Just sprinkle or pour in the ingredients and scrub.

✿ Place a few drops of liquid dish soap in the toilet, brush, and flush.

✿ Combine 1 cup of lemon juice and ½ cup of baking soda for a toilet with hard-water stains. Let sit for 30 minutes before flushing.

Miscellaneous Tips

✿ Add a chlorine filter to the showerhead(s). This is an inexpensive method of filtering out most of the chlorine normally present in household water.

✿ Use a drain protector/cover to prevent shower drain clogs.

✿ When buying a curtain liner for your tub, choose one that is PVC-free.

In the Laundry Room

Washing

- ☼ Use Borax as a laundry booster for particularly dirty loads.
- ☼ Add a cup of vinegar to the wash to keep colors looking bright and to keep your clothing soft.
- ☼ Add ¼ to ½ cup of baking soda to the beginning of the wash cycle to soften clothes and eliminate odors.
- ☼ Hydrogen peroxide is an environmentally friendly, antifungal, antiviral product. It also works well as a bleaching agent. For stains on light-colored fabric, soak in hydrogen peroxide (3% to 6% solution).

Drying/Dry Cleaning

- ☼ Stay away from conventional dryer sheets. Many contain a host of chemicals proven to have adverse impacts on human health.
- ☼ Seek out a green dry cleaner. Most conventional dry cleaners use a chemical solvent called perchloroethylene (perc), a probable human carcinogen with an array of both short- and long-term adverse health effects. Don't be afraid to ask your dry cleaner what type of equipment he or she uses, and if the equipment uses perc.
- ☼ Buy cotton garment bags and bring them to the dry cleaner to put your clean clothes in. This saves on plastic bags and enables the chemicals used during dry cleaning

> to dissipate (otherwise, the chemicals are trapped in the plastic bags and will eventually pollute the air in your closet at home).

✿ Wash wool and cashmere by hand.

Miscellaneous Tips

✿ Invest in a clothesline!

✿ If you are buying a new washer and/or dryer, opt for one with an Energy Star label. An appliance with this label has been designed to be extremely energy efficient.

Glossary

100% ORGANIC. A label indicating that a product contains only organically produced ingredients and processing aids. Organic foods are grown without synthetic fertilizers, pesticides, genetic engineering, growth hormones, irradiation, or antibiotics.

1,4 dioxane. A known animal carcinogen and probable human carcinogen that is the by-product of some manufacturing processes. It is also a skin and lung irritant and is widely believed to be toxic to the human nervous system and kidneys. 1,4 dioxane exists in numerous personal care products, and is used as a foaming agent.

acute health effect. Characterized by the rapid onset of symptoms. Often the symptoms subside when the exposure stops.

allergen. A substance that triggers an allergic reaction. Common allergens are dust, dust mites, pollen, and pet dander.

bioaccumulation. The result when a toxic substance is absorbed at a rate faster than it is excreted. The term is generally used to refer to toxins. Bioaccumulation tends to take place when the body is unable to expel toxins through sweat or urine, for example. Substances that bioaccumulate tend to be stored in the body's fat tissue, where they can remain for years. They may also be discharged in breast milk.

biodegradable. The ability to decompose naturally, often with the help of microorganisms.

body burden. The toxic chemicals, both naturally occurring and man-made, that exist in a person's body at a given point in time.

carcinogen. An agent that causes cancer. Carcinogens alter the information cells receive from their DNA, which causes immature cells to accumulate in the body (the immature cells do not function properly). There are natural and synthetic carcinogens.

central nervous system. The "control center" of the body, comprising the brain and the spinal cord.

chlorine. A naturally occurring element and a highly reactive gas. Chlorine is a serious eye, nose, and upper respiratory tract irritant.

chronic health effect. Brought about by repeated exposure over days, months, or years. Typically, chronic health effects do not present with immediate symptoms. Examples are lead and mercury poisoning, and cancer.

diethanolamine (DEA). A synthetic chemical used to produce lather in personal care products and cleaning agents. DEA can react with other ingredients to create the carcinogen nitrosodiethanolamine (NDEA). NDEA has been shown to be easily absorbed through the skin and is linked with various types of cancer. It has also been identified as a hormone disruptor.

DMDM hydantoin. A preservative that works by releasing formaldehyde into a product. It is widely used in shampoos, conditioners, and cosmetics to prevent the growth of bacteria, mold, and mildew. Formaldehyde is a known human carcinogen.

endocrine system. The system in the human body that regulates growth, development, metabolism, sexual function, and reproductive processes. This system is responsible for processes that happen slowly, such as cell growth.

genetically modified organism (GMO). A plant or animal whose genetic code has been altered to give it characteristics that it would not have naturally. Genetic altering is accomplished by splicing the gene of one organism into another in order to embed the receiving organism with a "desirable" trait.

hormone disruptor. A substance that when inhaled or otherwise consumed can alter the normal functioning of the endocrine system by blocking or mimicking hormones. Exposure to endocrine disruptors can have adverse biological effects, including impaired reproductive function, increased odds of certain cancers, and early onset of puberty.

MADE WITH ORGANIC INGREDIENTS. A label meaning that the product, usually food, contains at least 70 percent organic ingredients.

mercury/methylmercury. Naturally occurring heavy metals. In humans, mercury attacks the nervous system and the kidneys. Methylmercury forms when mercury is deposited into water (streams, river, lakes, oceans). Bacteria and other natural processes can convert mercury into methylmercury. Fetuses and young children are at the highest risk for mercury/methylmercury exposure because they are still developing. Health impacts of high exposure include serious neurological problems that share symptoms with cerebral palsy.

monoethanolamine (MEA). A chemical used as a foaming agent and stabilizer in cosmetics. MEA in an ammonia compound that can form dangerous nitrosamines (a class of chemicals, some of which are carcinogenic).

mutagen. An agent, such as a chemical, that can cause changes in the genetic code of a cell. Exposure to mutagens can have serious health consequences.

neurotoxin. A chemical that causes damage to the nervous system. Fetuses and children are particularly vulnerable to neurotoxin exposure.

ORGANIC. The green-and-white seal indicating that a food contains at least 95 percent organic ingredients. These foods have been grown without synthetic fertilizers, pesticides, genetic engineering, growth hormones, irradiation, or antibiotics.

parabens. Preservatives used in personal care products, designed to extend their shelf life and prevent the growth of bacteria. Parabens are known hormone disruptors. Some of the more common parabens found in cosmetics, foods, and drugs are *methylparaben*, *propylparaben*, *butylparaben*, and *benzylparaben*.

perchloroethylene (PERC). The toxic chemical used in conventional dry-cleaning operations. Long-term exposure to perc has been linked with cancer and damage to the central nervous system, the reproductive system, the liver, and the kidneys.

persistent bioaccumulative toxins (PBTs). Toxic substances, both naturally occurring and man-made, that are long-lasting in the environment and build up in the food chain to concentrations that pose risks to both human health and our ecosystem.

pesticide. Any substance that prevents, repels, or destroys pests. Many synthetic pesticides contain ingredients that are harmful to human health. Exposure to a number of traditional chemical pesticides is linked to asthma, skin rashes, emphysema, and cancer. Look for biologically based pesticides when addressing any pest issues.

petrochemicals. Chemicals derived from petroleum, natural gas, or coal. Generally speaking, the production of petroleum-based products is harder on the environment than is that of their plant-based counterparts. Plant-based products are biodegradable and made with renewable resources.

perfluorocarbons (PFCs). Chemical found in nonstick materials such as Teflon. In studies, PFCs have been linked to both hormone disruption and cancer. PFCs are some of the greenhouse gases declared dangerous to human health by the US Environmental Protection Agency.

phosphates. Minerals used in cleaning agents to soften water and increase the effectiveness of a product. Although phosphates don't appear to pose risks to human health, they do make their way into our wastewater, and it is here that they can lead to algal blooms, which choke off the oxygen supply to organisms in the water.

phthalates (pronounced THA-lates). A class of chemicals ubiquitous in many personal care and consumer products used primarily as plasticizers. Recent studies have shown that low-dose exposure to phthalates during certain windows of pregnancy can impact normal male sexual development. *Dibutyl* and *diethylhexyl* are two phthalates that are commonly found in cosmetics that have been banned in the European Union due to safety concerns.

polyethylene glycol (PEG). Skin-cleansing agents and conditioners that are used widely in cosmetics. Polyethylene glycol compounds (PEG-6, PEG-150, etc.) are synthetic chemicals that have been linked with various types of cancer and other adverse health effects.

polychlorinated biphenyls (PCBs). A class of highly toxic synthetic chemicals manufactured in North America from 1929 to 1979. Manufacturing was banned then because of the adverse health effects of exposure to PCBs and their persistence in the environment. Exposure to PCBs has been connected with skin and liver toxicity and cancer.

sodium lauryl sulfate (SLS)/sodium laureth sulfate (SLES). Two synthetic chemicals widely used as foaming agents in personal care and cleaning agents (and in engine degreasers and floor cleaners). As Renée Loux writes in her book *Easy Green Living*, both SLS and SLES are skin irritants and decrease the skin's immune response. SLES is frequently contaminated with *dioxane*, which is a known carcinogen. SLS, which is readily absorbed by the body, is a suspected endocrine disruptor.

triethanolamine (TEA). An ammonia compound used as a stabilizing agent in many personal care products. It can form dangerous nitrosamines when mixed with other ingredients, and has been shown to be an eye and skin irritant and an allergen.

teratogen. An agent (chemical, infectious disease, or pollutant) that interferes with the normal development of a fetus. Exposure to teratogens can result in the loss of the fetus, pregnancy complications, and birth defects.

triclosan. A pesticide with a long list of adverse effects on human health. Exposure can lead to antibiotic resistance and kidney and liver damage, and can disrupt the normal functioning of the thyroid. Triclosan degrades into *dioxins* and *chlorophenols*, both of which are known carcinogens.

toxin. A poisonous substance capable of causing disease when introduced to tissues in the body.

ureas. A class of preservatives that can release formaldehyde in small amounts. These are linked to contact dermatitis.

volatile organic compound (VOC). Gases emitted from a wide variety of common household items, such as furniture, paint, and shower curtains. VOCs diminish the quality of our air, both indoors and out, and are linked to asthma and other respiratory problems as well as cancer. Keeping your home well ventilated is an effective way to minimize the VOC concentration indoors.

Notes

Introduction

1. Ken Cook, "10 Americans," Environmental Working Group Web site, http://www.ewg.org/kidsafe.
2. "Making Chemicals Safe for Kids: Senate Panel Will Examine 'Broken' Toxics Law," Environmental Working Group, http://www.ewg.org/node/27137.

Labeling

1. Marion Nestle, *What to Eat* (New York: North Point Press, 2006), 39.

Section I: Food

1. World Health Organization, "The Top 10 Causes of Death, 2004," http://www.who.int/mediacentre/factsheets/fs310/en.
2. Michael Pollan, *In Defense of Food* (New York: The Penguin Press, 2008), 90.
3. Ibid., 145.
4. Ibid., 1.
5. Marion Nestle, *What to Eat* (New York: North Point Press, 2006), 517.

6. Michael Pollan, *In Defense of Food* (New York: The Penguin Press, 2008), 164.

7. Marion Nestle, *What to Eat* (New York: North Point Press, 2006), 39.

8. Ibid., 52.

Chapter 1: Produce

1. Joni Mitchell, "Big Yellow Taxi," *Ladies of the Canyon*, Warner Brothers, 1970.

Chapter 2: Dairy

1. Andrew G. Renehan, at al., "Insulin-like growth factor (IGF)-I, IGF Binding Protein-3, and Cancer Risk: Systematic Review and Meta-regression Analysis," *The Lancet* 363:9418 (2004): 1346–53.

Chapter 4: Dairy

1. Sustainable Table, "Artificial Hormones," www.sustainabletable.org/issues/hormones.

Chapter 6: Genetically Modified Organisms

1. Institute for Responsible Technology, 2008, "State of the Science on the Health Risks of GM Foods," www.responsibletechnology.org/utility/showArticle/?objectID=18.

2. About the Author, "Author Bio for Jeffrey M. Smith," Seeds of Deception, www.seedsofdeception.com/utility/showArticle/?objectID=15.

Section II: Personal Care Products

1. Renée Loux, *Easy Green Living* (New York: Rodale, 2008), 70.

2. Ibid., 168.

3. Donella Meadows, *Global Citizen* (Washington, D.C.: Island Press, 1991),165.

Chapter 7: Children's Personal Care Products

1. Leonardo Trasande, Testimony before U.S. Senate Environment and Public Works Committee, September 16, 2008.

2. Sheela Sathyanarayana, et al., "Baby Care Products: Possible Sources of Infant Phthalate Exposure," *Pediatrics* 121:2 (2008): 260–68.

3. Environmental Working Group's Skin Deep Cosmetics Safety Database, "EWG Summary: Safety Guide to Children's Personal Care Products," www.cosmeticsdatabase.com/special/parentsguide/summary.php.

4. Environmental Working Group's Skin Deep Cosmetics Safety Database, "Sunscreen Summary— What Works and What's Safe," www.cosmeticsdatabase.com/special/sunscreens2008/summary.php.

5. Philip Landrigan, Mary Landrigan, and Herbert Needleman, *Raising Healthy Children in a Toxic World* (Emmaus, PA: Rodale, 2001), 15.

Chapter 8: Hair Care

1. Lyndsey Layton, "Probable Carcinogens Found in Baby Toiletries," *The Washington Post*, March 13, 2009.

2. Renée Loux, *Easy Green Living* (New York: Rodale, 2008), 193.

3. Yawei Zhang, et al., "Personal Use of Hair Dye and the Risk of Certain Subtypes of Non-Hodgkin Lymphoma," *American Journal of Epidemiology* 167 (April 2008): 1321–31.

4. R. Baan, K. Straif, Y. Grosse, B. Secretan, "Carcinogenicity of Some Aromatic Amines, Organic Dyes, and Related Exposures," *The Lancet Oncology* volume 9, issue 4 (April 2008): 322–23.

5. Renée Loux, *Easy Green Living* (New York: Rodale, 2008), 201.

6. Sheela Sathyanarayana, et al., "Baby Care Products: Possible Sources of Infant Phthalate Exposure," *Pediatrics* 121:2 (2008): 260–68.

Chapter 9: Skin Care

1. Deirdre Imus, *Green This* (New York: Simon & Schuster, 2007), 86.

2. Ibid., *The Essential Green You* (New York: Simon & Schuster, 2009), 105.

3. P. D. Darbre, A. Aljarrah, W. R. Miller, N. G. Coldham, M. J. Sauer and G. S. Pope, "Concentrations of Parabens in Human Breast Tumours," *Journal of Applied Toxicology* 24 (Jan. 2004): 5–13.

Chapter 10: Oral Care

1. Green Your: Your Green Guide to Living, "Mouthwash," www.greenyour.com/body/personal-care/mouthwash.

Chapter 11: Cosmetics

1. Sophie Uliano, *Gorgeously Green* (New York: HarperCollins, 2008), 54.

Chapter 12: Indoor Air Quality

1. Mikki Halpin and Linda Hunter, *Green Clean* (New York: Melcher Media, 2005), 85.

Chapter 13: The Kitchen

1. Renée Loux, *Easy Green Living* (New York: Rodale, 2008), 52.

2. Ibid., 54.

Chapter 14: The Bathroom

1. Deirdre Imus, *Green This* (New York: Simon & Schuster, 2007), 44.

2. Karen Logan, *Clean Earth, Clean Planet* (New York: Pocket Books, 1997), 235.

3. Mikki Halpin and Linda Hunter, *Green Clean* (New York: Melcher Media, 2005), 75.

4. "Economic Impact Analysis of the Hydrochloric Acid (HCl) Production NESHAP." US Office of Air Quality Planning and Standards, Environmental Protection Agency, February 2003.

5. Karen Logan, *Clean Earth, Clean Planet* (New York: Pocket Books, 1997), 228.

6. Ibid., 229.

7. Philip Landrigan, Mary Landrigan, and Herbert Needleman, *Raising Healthy Children in a Toxic World* (Emmaus, PA: Rodale, 2001), 27.

Chapter 15: The Laundry

1. Natural Resources Defense Council, "Endocrine Dispruptors," http://www.nrdc.org/health/effects/qendoc.asp.

2. Ibid.

3. Richard Stahlhut, et al., "Concentrations of Urinary Phthalate Metabolites Are Associated with Increased Waist Circumference and Insulin Resistance in Adult U.S. Males," *Environmental Health Perspectives* 115:6 (2008): 877–82.

4. Canadian Centre for Occupational Health and Safety, "Health Effects of Benzene," www.ccohs.ca/oshanswers/chemicals/chem_profiles/benzene/health_ben.html.

5. Renée Loux, *Easy Green Living* (New York: Rodale, 2008), 245.

Resources

Design for the Environment (www.epa.gov/dfe)

Environmental Defense Fund (www.edf.org)

Environmental Working Group (www.ewg.org)

Environmental Working Group, Shopper's Guide to Produce (www.foodnews.org)

Environmental Working Group, Skin Deep Cosmetic Safety Database (www.cosmeticsdatabase.com)

Greening Your Family (www.greeningyourfamily.com *and* www.lindseycarmichael.net)

Local Harvest (www.localharvest.org)

Natural Products Association (www.naturalproductsassoc. org)

Natural Resources Defense Council (www.nrdc.org)

Natural Solutions (www.naturalsolutionsmag.com)

The Campaign for Safe Cosmetics (www.safecosmetics.org)

The Cornucopia Institute (www.cornucopia.org)

United States Department of Agriculture (www.usda.gov)

United States Environmental Protection Agency (www.epa. gov)

Whole Foods Market Web site (www.wholefoodsmarket. com)

About the Author

Lindsey Carmichael graduated from the University of Vermont with a bachelor's degree in English and earned a master's degree from the University of New Hampshire in public health. She has worked in the healthcare field for fifteen years and is a frequent speaker about healthy, "green" living.

While in graduate school, Lindsey's eyes were opened to the disturbing reality that many of the products we consume contain ingredients known to pose a threat to human health, particularly the health of children. Her role as mother to a young child fueled her desire to create a resource guide to make it easy for others to identify safe food and personal care and cleaning products. Lindsey lives on the New Hampshire seacoast with her husband and son.

Index

ADHD. *See* attention deficit hyperactivity disorder
air quality, 67–69, 77, 79
Albuterol, x
alcohol, 59
allergies, 35
all-purpose cleaners, 70–72, 77–78, 89
aluminum compounds, 52–53
Alzheimer's disease, 1, 49, 52–53
American Dental Association, 38
American Journal of Epidemiology, 46
ammonia compounds, 30, 54, 71, 75, 76, 78, 79
ammonium chloride, 86
animal testing, 30
antibacterial compounds, 30, 35
ANTIBIOTIC FREE label, xiv
antibiotics

in dairy products, xiv, 12–13
in meat, 18–20
in water supplies, 22
antimicrobial soaps, 49
antiperspirants, 52–54
asbestos, 42
attention deficit hyperactivity disorder (ADHD), x

baby powder, 41–42
baby wipes, 40–41
Badge-40H, xi
bathroom cleaning products, 77–81, 91–92
benzene, 68, 69, 84
benzophenone-3, 55
BHA. *See* butylated hydroxyanisole
biodegradable products, 71
birth defects, x, 50, 63, 72
bisphenol-A, 83
bladder cancer, 22, 46
bleach products, 85–86, 93

109

Readers' Comments

"When considering the breadth of options for cleaning products, food selections, and personal care products, *Greening Your Family*, is an invaluable resource for families and individuals who want to make informed decisions when purchasing safe, eco-friendly food and products that are part of daily living. Ms. Carmichael's easy-to-read book not only provides a listing of recommended products but also includes which products could be utilized for various household tasks; where the consumer may purchase the products; and numerous web-based resources for additional information. *Greening Your Family* is an essential guide to anyone who is looking to minimize the impact of chemicals on their lives."

   —Rosemary M. Caron, PhD, MPH, Associate Professor and MPH Program Director, Department of Health Management and Policy, University of New Hampshire

"As a mother and health care provider, I was relieved to find this realistic guide to keeping one's family safe. Carmichael provides well-researched, practical answers to the questions

we all have about avoidable toxins in our everyday lives. As I began reading, I was struck by how I could immediately use her suggestions in my household and workplace. This is a "must-read" for anyone interested in improving the health of themselves, their loved ones and society as a whole. An enjoyable, invaluable resource that is sure to become your "go-to" reference for years to come."
　—*Jill Capobianco ARNP, Medical Director, Families First of the Greater Seacoast, Mobile Healthcare Van*

"An easy read with compelling advice. Carmichael has a balanced approach in supporting her advice with scientific detail and wrapping up the take home message with a large brush stroke of how to take the first step. Her dialogue with the reader is engaging, and one can skim the surface of practicality or dive deeper with the research behind her summaries. A great bridal shower / baby shower gift as it ranks in the ABC's of setting up house and creating a healthy, eco-friendly environment for those that live in it. A 'must have' reference guide for any individual or family."
　—*Elisabeth Robinson RNC, MS, Family Nurse Practitioner*